MAKING
Mechanical Toys

Rodney Peppé

The Crowood Press

for Tatjana my wife

In appreciation of her help and encouragement and typing
a manuscript which, without plans, made little sense.

'This is a book of ideas and whenever it inspires other ideas it will have value'
Roger Hill and Orson Welles, *Everybody's Shakespeare* (Todd Press, 1934)

First published in 2005 by
The Crowood Press Ltd
Ramsbury, Marlborough
Wiltshire SN8 2HR

www.crowood.com

British Library Cataloguing-in-Publication Data
A catalogue record for this book is available from the British Library.

ISBN 1 86126 723 1

Typefaces used: M Plantin (main text and captions); Melior (labelling).

Typeset and designed by D & N Publishing
Lambourn Woodlands, Hungerford, Berkshire.

Printed and bound in Malaysia by Times Offset (M) Sdn. Bhd.

CONTENTS

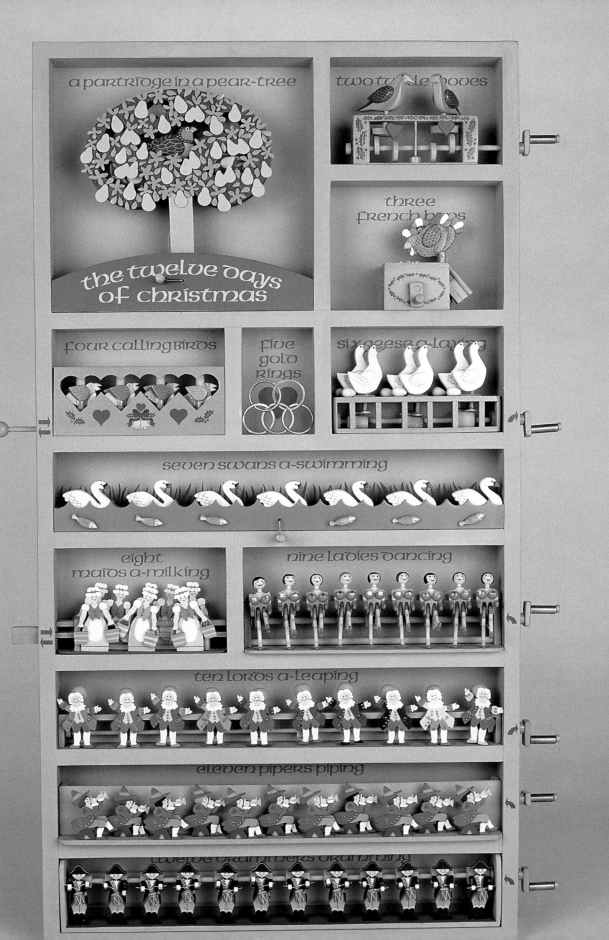

PREFACE

By definition, toys are for children; but they can also be for adults – certainly, mechanical toys have a universal appeal which transcends categories of age. The fascination lies in simple automated movement, whether the mechanism is hidden or revealed. One has only to visit an automata and mechanical toys exhibition to realize the truth of this. It is a different attraction to the one that exists for dolls and model cars which imitate life in their scaled-down forms, reflecting surrogate relationships for real life counterparts. The cycle of movement, however simple, in a mechanical toy allows us to control the motive magic by just turning a crank handle. We are our own magicians and therein lies the fascination.

The main differences distinguishing automata from mechanical toys are the running time and number of cams: to put it in a nutshell, automata are devised to execute a series of complicated movements within a time span. The duration and complexity of the cycle distinguishes them from the simpler mechanical toys. Although toys such as those described in this book are widely referred to as automata they are, by the foregoing definition, mechanical toys. The mechanisms of these toys are comparatively simple and they are quite happy to be designated thus.

Makers spend many hours designing and building mechanical toys, many of which are one-offs. It is not surprising then that they become, in the main, gallery toys for collectors and so could be termed elite toys for elitists. In this book I want to remove the 'elite' label and make mechanical toys available to everyone, including children who cannot afford to buy such pieces shown in exhibitions. By looking at the plans and photographs and reading the instructions any of the toys in this book can be reproduced to perform as described and give pleasure to both the maker and recipient.

However, I would not wish to give free licence to cottage industrial toymakers to sell these pieces on the open market. That is certainly not my intention. My granddaughter, on learning that I was doing this book, asked her parents why Grandpa was giving away his designs? A perspicacious question from a bright seven-year-old but I would rather admit to sharing than to giving away my designs. After all, sharing my work with a wider audience is a concept I'm comfortable and familiar with, since I share my stories and illustrations from my children's books and TV series.

Some automatists and makers of mechanical toys transpose their three-dimensional work into paper or wooden kits. There are a number of excellent examples on the market. In this way these designers have devised a way of making their work more accessible to a wider public. They, too, are sharing their work, giving opportunities to budding automatists to build mechanical toys. Just as I would not expect to buy one of their made-up kits as their original work, I would not expect to find my creations in this book passed off as either my original work or that of the reader. It's a question of trust between author and reader.

More than twenty years ago, I published a book, now out of print, *Rodney Peppé's Moving Toys*. Over that period I have had an intermittent correspondence with readers who have made toys from plans and photographs in the book and sent photographs of their versions. One reader, I remember, sent miniaturized copies of the moving toys which did him credit and pleased me as the unwitting instigator of his project. More sadly, I received letters from a reader in France suffering from a chronic illness. The book had lifted his spirits in the face of adversity, which was gratifying to me. So there are advantages in sharing one's work, although still I wince if I see it, albeit in surrogate form, optimistically priced on market stalls.

Making Mechanical Toys is a book for anyone wishing to make a special toy for a special person. The 'hearts and flowers' element is catered for in several pieces which would make beautiful Valentine's Day presents. These are 'Love Birds', which are based on a section in my 'Twelve Days of Christmas' (*see* illustration opposite); the 'Elephant Messenger', who flies above the clouds holding a Valentine's card in his trunk; 'Two-headed Strongman',

Rodney Peppé's 'The Twelve Days of Christmas'
838 × 432 × 57mm (33 × 16.96 × 2.25in). Three of the mechanical toys in this book are based on this piece: these are 'Love Birds'; 'The Bluebelles'; and 'Drummer'.

a surrealist idea based on a painting by Magritte; and 'Dancing Charlie', who carries a bouquet for his beloved. There is also an exciting 'Kim' game to be played with 'Jungle Box', where the animals appear one by one in the jungle. And there's lots of fun to be had with the cat-and-mouse piece, 'MIAOW!', where the cat never quite catches the mouse who is after the cheese. Dancing ladies, 'Different Drummers', bobbing boats and a snappy little alligator clothes-peg toy jostle for attention in what proposes itself to be an unequalled opportunity to make mechanical toys.

All the toys were made especially for this book, one after the other, without a break. The plans were drawn concurrently with each toy so there is a visible homogeneity about the pieces without them falling into a particular signature style. They are original designs which have not, with one exception, been sold elsewhere. The exception is the 'Elephant Messenger', a version of which was sold with five other of my pieces to the Arima Toys and Automata Museum in Kobe, Japan. The themes and influences that overlie the designs are to be found in the areas of graphic design and children's books; not unnaturally, since these are domains in which I have been active over the years.

A bit of helpful advice might be to tackle the pieces in sustained periods, when you can concentrate, following the plans step-by-step, rather than letting long periods elapse before you return to the project in hand. Remember, as Lloyd-George once said: 'You can't cross a chasm in two small steps.'

Happy landings!

INTRODUCTION

This book is a companion to *Automata and Mechanical Toys* (The Crowood Press, 2002) which features modern makers and describes, with plans and photographs, how to make the main mechanisms to be found in automata. It seemed to be a natural step to follow this up with a book giving examples of mechanical toys and instructions on how to make them. The books complement one another and for those readers who made some of the mechanisms from the first book, the second goes the extra mile by offering seventeen toymaking projects for readers to sink their teeth into. Dental bridgework not withstanding, my sincere hope is that both old and new readers will derive as much pleasure from making the toys as I had in designing and constructing them.

No account of mechanical toys would be complete without mentioning the renowned Cabaret Mechanical Theatre and its artists under the auspices of Sue Jackson, its founder and her daughter, Sarah Alexander. Leading automatists Paul Spooner, Peter Markey, Ron Fuller and Keith Newstead have, with their own individual styles, lit creative beacons over the years which still burn brightly today for others to follow. From a different direction comes Frank Nelson, who is probably the closest link to the classic French automatists of the nineteenth century. Other luminaries in the field such as Tony Mann, Bob Race, Tim Hunkin, Andy Hazell and Jan Zalud have, among others too numerous to mention, left indelible traces of their talent in this magical area of toymaking which is becoming ever more widely known and popular.

Both as a creative source and an outlet for mechanical toymakers, Ian McKay and Fleur Hitchcock provided a selling venue for years at Hitchcocks' in Bath. They have put this on hold while bringing up a young family, but continue to sell from their Barn at Limpley Stoke, Bath, and run Mechanical Toymaking courses with the occasional exhibition. Other automata and toymaking courses are run at Timberkits 'Machinations' in Powys, mid-Wales by Eric and Alison Williamson. In London, 'Automatamania', run by Michael and Maria Start in Gray's Antique Market, by the Bond Street Tube, is well worth a visit.

One figure whose influence on modern automata and mechanical toys spreads like a mantle over a quarter of a century is the artist-craftsman Sam Smith (1908–83). Many modern makers acknowledge Smith as their hero even though he himself was not actually an automatist (beyond making very special jumping jacks). He is often referred to as the father of modern automata, inspiring other makers with his artistry, creativity and superb craftsmanship, both as a carver and painter.

He was also the most generous of men, encouraging makers Peter Markey and Frank Nelson whom he admired. They in their turn inspired others and so the wheel goes round. Another strong influence is Alexander Calder (1898–1976), famed internationally for his large mobiles. He produced, over the years, a cork-and-wire circus (with himself as self-appointed ringmaster) which eventually filled five suitcases. Douglas Wilson, who works in wire, acknowledges Calder's influence together with that of the wire toys made by children in many African countries.

There is little that connects the automata and mechanical toys of today to those of the past. Yet somehow their provenance in the late nineteenth century is important if only to realize that their exclusivity was very similar to that which obtains today. They were adult toys, not for the nursery, though they were placed in children's sections in exhibitions. Automata became more and more sophisticated and increasingly lifelike, inevitably pricing themselves out of the market. Perhaps too much realism cheated the imagination, for mechanical toys with simpler mechanisms and less stories to tell, so to speak, flourished. They survived social pressures, changing fashions and unpredictable market trends.

If modern gallery mechanical toys have little to do with late nineteenth-century toys they have even less connection to the jumping pigs, barking dogs, twirling pussycats and somersaulting rodents we see today in department stores and toyshops. Their mechanisms are extremely ingenious and far beyond the scope of gallery toys. Much closer forebears are the cheap wooden toys of the 1820s sold in a shop in London called Edlin's

Rational Repository of Amusement and Instruction. These were simple little movable toys made of wood and cloth with very basic mechanisms (no more than a cam, a bit of wire and some leather) depicting household activities such as spinning, snuff taking and the like.

The main difference is that whereas those old toys were carved and crudely clothed, the mechanical toys found in galleries and shops today have fairly flat wooden components painted or left bare. It's true that the old toys would not have sported anything as advanced as a Geneva wheel in its workings for example, so our mechanical toys – the gallery variety – are perhaps a little more advanced, but not much.

Having settled into a new century in a world where international telecommunications are instantaneous and global travel is undertaken in hours, we must ask ourselves if the making of simple mechanical toys, without using modern technology, is at all relevant. A robot,

fed on a diet of chips, is in a far better position to perform motive marvels than is our mechanical toy. It is, of course, precisely that lack of technology in the face of cold electronic efficiency, which appeals to the champions of the modern mechanical toy.

Who are these champions? They are the makers who, as artists, merely want to make their art move a little. They are the collectors who, in a financially anaemic field, see antiques of the future. They are the schoolchildren who undertake design and technology activities through the National Curriculum. They are the students who want to follow in the footsteps of Cabaret Mechanical Theatre. They are those who, having once been children themselves, have retained a child's fascination for simple, ingenious movement. And they are those who make time to take a break from the rapidity of everyday modern living and enjoy the simple quirkiness and wit of a mechanical toy.

While automata in the late nineteenth century became increasingly sophisticated and lifelike, pricing themselves out of the market, mechanical toys like these illustrated here survived social pressures, fashions and unpredictable market trends.

HOW TO USE THIS BOOK

The first step when making any toy will be to check that you have the materials required. Measurements are given slightly oversized on the materials panels to allow for handling dowels and cutting panels. If you cannot obtain the materials stipulated, others can easily be substituted. Say, for example, that stripwood is suggested but it is not available to you, then exchange it for plywood of the same measurements. If the thickness is not quite correct, make adjustments; but ensure that any alterations made are compatible with the specifications of the other materials.

It is essential that you read the instructions together with the plans. When the instructions tell you to cut from plywood, the actual thickness is given to you in millimetres on the plans. This relieves the instructions of too many measurements except for the widths of drilled holes, which are shown visually on the plans.

The term 'temporarily bonded' is frequently used and means that two pieces of plywood have been fastened together with sticky tape or dabs of glue which can later be removed. This may be useful, for example, when you wish to drill two side panels together to make an accurate bearing for a crankshaft.

When multiple pieces are cut, whether together or not, they are denoted by an '×' on the plans preceding the quantity to show the number of pieces to cut.

Once a plan number has been given within the instructions, it is not referred to again until a different plan is required. Thus items to be cut out are all on one plan, unless another plan number is mentioned.

GENERAL NOTES

Transferring designs from this book is mainly done by using photocopies spray-glued to plywood and then cut out as instructed. Use only the minimum amount of glue, as the photocopies are to be peeled off once the designs have been cut out. If they are difficult to remove, white spirit or lighter fuel can be used to loosen them, but take care not to rub the design while wet.

Three of the toys have designs which are copied (two in colour) and retained as the surface design spray-glued

to plywood. In these cases, of course, the bonding must be permanent and both surfaces, the back of the print and plywood, should be spray-glued, bonded together and firmly burnished down.

There are instances when you will need to transfer the design by hand. Trace the design onto tracing paper with an HB pencil. Offset the tracing by burnishing it onto another piece of tracing paper and burnish this down onto the wood. The image is not then reversed.

Shaft bearings are shown 1mm (0.04in) wider than the shaft's diameter, to allow for shrinkage after painting. Although a 6mm diameter dowel shaft will turn adequately in a 6.5mm bearing, this will become too tight after painting.

When **fixing cams to shafts**, initially they should be friction fitted by using a bearing with the same diameter as the shaft itself. The cams are tight enough to be tested and repositioned but would, in time, become loose on the shaft. When the piece is finally assembled, either glue the area the cam is going to cover, or superglue all around the edge of the cams where they touch the shaft.

Scoring plywood with a craft knife when cutting straight lines provides a guide channel for the scroll saw or fret saw to follow.

Panels should be cut at least 5mm (0.20in) larger than the measurements specified to allow the photocopy to be applied to the plywood and cut out. Use a jigsaw to cut them out roughly.

Drilling collets is made easier if you make a slight central hole with a bradawl for the drill bit to find and settle into. Grip the collet with pliers or a mole wrench to prevent it spinning round in your fingers.

If **dowels** are to be thinned, use a craft knife to scrape away the excess before sanding.

TOOLS

It is assumed that the reader has a basic set of tools, including a powered scroll saw or fretsaw for making small tightly curved cuts in wood up to 19mm (0.75in) thick. You will also require a jigsaw for cutting out plywood which is too long for the throats of the other saws.

Other tools which you may find useful are listed below:

- A mitre box is a hand-operated metallic device which guides the saw in cutting accurate mitre and right-angle joints. A mitre saw is recommended for the best results where the saw is integrated with the box.
- A power belt sander is ideal for making boxes and squaring-off edges before manually sanding or chamfering them off. It runs a continuous belt around two rollers. Be very careful to keep fingers away from the metal parts where the belt runs through.
- A sanding disc is an attachment for a power drill, made of rubber with a steel shank. It will leave cross-grain scratches but reduces wood quickly. It is much cheaper than a belt sander and good for filing off panel pins on pin wheels.
- A pin hammer is useful for tapping in panel pins and dowel into plywood or stripwood.
- Snipe-nosed pliers are useful for gripping small objects in confined spaces.
- Diagonal wire cutters will be needed for cutting wire close to the surface.
- Mole grips (or wrenches) are ideal for a wide variety of workbench eventualities, ranging from removing stubborn dowels from cranks to gripping collets to prevent them from spinning when drilled.

The following types of knives may be useful:

- A surgeon's scalpel with a variety of blades (especially No. 11) is very good for light duty, very precise, cutting.
- A trimming or craft knife has disposable blades which can be stored in its housing. A retractable blade has a safety advantage.
- A putty knife is an invaluable tool for prizing apart temporarily bonded pieces of plywood if glued in spot areas. (Otherwise, tape is used for bonding.) A spatula will do the same job.
- Awls and bradawls are used for making starter holes for screws and nails in wood. Always twist them into wood and take care not to press too hard or the wood will split.

MATERIALS

The main materials required for making each toy are listed at the beginning of each chapter. The basic materials used to construct the toys described in this book are plywood, Aeroply, battening (PSE), stripwood, softwood and dowel. Additional materials, such as pop rivets and piano wire, will also be required for some toys.

Birch ply is the best plywood. Check the edges of ply board for gaps that have been filled but, nevertheless, run right through the board. When buying battening (PSE), or any softwood, watch out for splits and knots. Although these are often found in deal, it is otherwise a very nice wood to work with. Stripwood is made from hardwood, as are dowels. Birch dowels are best for rods and shafts as they don't bend. Try to buy dowels in batches as they can vary in diameter from batch to batch.

PRIMING AND PAINTING

All the toys in this book were painted with acrylic craft colours with a primer of matt white vinyl emulsion. If you want to use casein emulsion paints such as Plaka colour, use ordinary matt white emulsion as a primer. A primer not only seals the surface of the wood, it gives subsequent coats of paint a lustrous base to enhance them. The colours are waterproof when dry.

Two or three coats of paint should be applied, as required, on top of the primer. Sand down lightly between coats. Varnishing and lacquering are not necessary for acrylic colours which have a built-in protective finish with a slight sheen. However, Plaka colours do need such protection to enhance their velvety-matt surfaces. Remember that colours darken with varnishing or lacquering.

Stencilling will be necessary when making one or two of the pieces featured in this book. The first step is to take a photocopy of the design and spray-glue the back so that it can be attached to a blank sheet of paper. Cut out the stencil from the reinforced paper print. Lightly coat the back of the stencil with spray glue and lay it gently on the surface to be stencilled. With a stencil brush or short-haired stiff-bristled brush dab paint into the stencil. One or two more coats will probably be needed to achieve full opacity. When the design has been successfully applied to the piece, carefully remove the stencil.

Sponging is done wet or dry. Cut a 50mm (2in) square sponge and dab it into a saucer with undiluted acrylic (or other) paint to produce a dry, well defined, leafy effect as on 'Jungle Box', the stone effect on 'Drummer', or the cloud effect on 'Elephant Messenger'. A mottled watery effect is achieved by wet sponging, as on 'Ark Toy' and 'Boat and Three Fish'.

Staining is effective if you want the wood grain to show through. Use diluted paint or coloured inks, and sand lightly when dry. 'American Sailboat' is an example of staining.

Brushes may be cleaned with soap and lukewarm water after using the waterbound paints which are recommended for these toys. If you are using oil or spirit-bound paints, brushes should be cleaned with white spirit or lighter fuel and then washed with soap in lukewarm water. Ensure that all traces of pigment are removed, otherwise old paint will build up and harden around the metal holder.

MAKING A BOX

Cutting out the box

1 Cut out the top panel A from plywood. Unless you wish to make a box with a lid, drill eight 1mm (0.04in) holes as indicated.
2 Cut out the base panel B from plywood.
3 Cut out the two side panels C from plywood. Drill seven 1mm (0.04in) holes in each of them.
4 Cut out the front and back panels D from plywood. Drill three 1mm (0.04in) holes as indicated.

Assembling the box

1 Tap in three 22mm (0.87in)-long panel pins into the pilot holes in the front and back panels D.
2 Place the base panel B flat against a block of wood supported by the bench stops on a work bench. Another block of wood, which is square to the work, should be placed on top of the base panel and held square to the front panel D, which is held against it.
3 Holding the supporting block, pin and glue the three panel pins in front panel D into the side edge of the base panel B as indicated by the dotted line on D.
4 Do likewise for the back panel D, which is pinned and glued into the opposite edge of the base panel B.
5 Tap in seven panel pins around each of the outer edges of the side panels C, except the top edges, as indicated.
6 Pin and glue the seven panel pins in one side panel into the side edge of the base panel B and the front edges of the front and back panels C as indicated.
7 Do likewise for the other side panel C. You now have a box without a lid.
8 Unless you want to make a box with a lid, tap eight panel pins into the pilot holes marked on the top panel A.
9 Pin and glue the panel pins around the edges, as marked, into the top edges of the other four panels.
10 If you want to make a box with a lid from this exercise, add a couple of hinges along one long edge of the top panel.
11 Sand off and chamfer the edges.

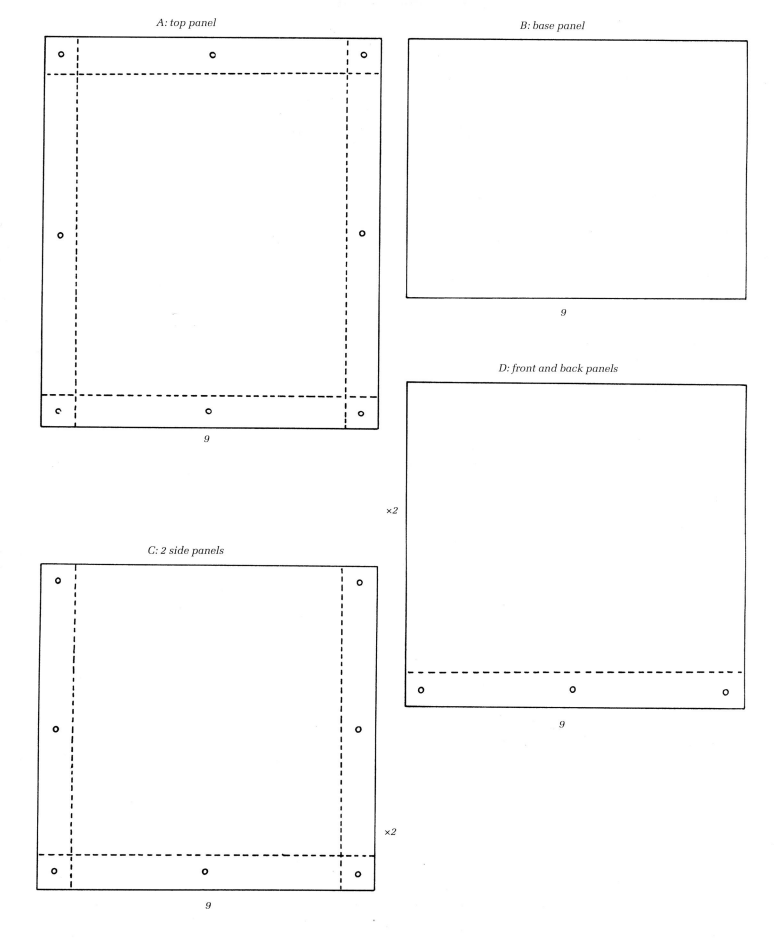

A: top panel

9

B: base panel

9

C: 2 side panels

×2

9

D: front and back panels

×2

9

1 NODDING ACQUAINTANCES

An homage to the American folk-art tradition of wind-powered whirligigs, this piece breaks the rules somewhat by being both hand-cranked and quite small. It acknowledges the 'special relationship' sometimes said to exist between America and Great Britain. It makes a nice shelf piece, although it is not strictly a whirligig, which is a garden ornament.

Because of the intricate nature of the decoration, colour photocopy the coloured drawings of the figures on the plans, spray-glue them onto Aeroply and cut them out. Alternatively, you may wish to trace the figures yourself. Only two other instances of cutting out photocopies occur in this book: *Dancing Charlie*, which is in black and white, and *Jungle Box*, with coloured animals.

MATERIALS

AEROPLY	407 × 407 × 1.5mm (16 × 16 × 0.06in)	Figures and paddles
PLYWOOD	135 × 80 × 11mm (5.32 × 3.15 × 0.43in)	Base
	240 × 60 × 6mm (9.45 × 2.36 × 0.24in)	Two bearing supports and crank
BATTENING (PSE)	135 × 23 × 23mm (5.32 × 0.91 × 0.91in)	Plinth
	20 × 20 × 20mm (0.79 × 0.79 × 0.79in)	Paddle block
DOWEL	41 × 6mm (1.62 × 0.24in)	Handle
	50 × 16mm (1.97 × 0.63in)	Three collets
PIANO WIRE	165 × 2mm (6.5 × 0.08in)	Crankshaft
FOUR POP RIVETS		Limb fixings

Making the base and plinth

1 Cut out the base from plywood, Plan 1, A.
2 Cut out the plinth from battening (PSE), Plan 1, B.
3 Lightly mark the positions for the feet, indicated by the dotted lines on the plinth.
4 Glue the plinth B, to the base A, as indicated by the dotted line. The dotted lines beyond the area of the plinth are for positioning the bearing supports later.

Nodding Acquaintances. 203 × 135 × 165mm (8 × 5.32 × 6.49in).

Spray-gluing prints and Aeroply

1 Cut the Aeroply into four equal pieces.
2 Colour photocopy plans 2 and 3 twice so that you have prints for the front and back of each figure.
3 Take two pieces of Aeroply and spray-glue the backs of one set of prints and the Aeroply. Allow the glue to become tacky before proceeding to the next stage.
4 Lay the prints from Plan 2, A–K down on the glued surface of the ply, smoothing them by hand. Place a protective sheet of paper over the prints and burnish them down firmly using a chamfered piece of batten (PSE).
5 Take one of the two blank pieces of Aeroply and temporarily bond it to one of the illustrated pieces with tape or dabs of glue so that the two sheets can be cut simultaneously. Do the same with the remaining two pieces.

Cutting out the figures and paddles

1 Cut out the figures and paddles, being careful to keep on or just inside the black line. To leave the line visible would be unsightly.
2 Keep the off-cuts, which will be held together at the narrow channel between the bodies and legs. They will serve as accurate guides for registering the reverse sides of the designs.

Registering the backs of the designs

1 Now it is time to use the second set of prints, Plan 3, A–J, to complete the backs of the figures and paddles. You will need to see the images through the paper so they can be registered accurately onto the backs of the pieces already cut. Ideally, a light box should be used but failing this a well-lit window will serve, with the aid of sticky tape.
2 Place the photocopy or colourcopy of Plan 3, A–J, face down and spray-glue the back fairly liberally, but be careful not to flood the spray. The glue is spread on the back of the photocopy rather than on the cut pieces in order to avoid getting any glue on the edges of the cut pieces, as this would make later painting difficult.
3 Place Plan 3, A–J face down on the light box (tacky side up), taped in position so that it does not slip.
4 Carefully place the matching off-cuts, now separated, onto the glued paper using the image of the design seen through the paper to locate the off-cuts in the correct position. Don't press down on the off-cuts or they may stick to the paper.
5 With the off-cuts exactly registered with the see-through designs, place the pieces into their corresponding shapes. Press them down firmly without touching the off-cuts.
6 Carefully peel away the off-cuts from the glued surface.
7 Turn over the glued sheet with the decorated parts stuck to it and firmly burnish them down with a protective layer of paper in between, as before.

Cutting away the waste

1 Using a very sharp scalpel or craft knife, cut away the waste so that the pieces have perfectly registered images on both sides.
2 Burnish down the sharp edges, gently sanding them down.

Colouring the pieces

1 The inks or watercolours used should be translucent so that the black-traced drawing shows through clearly. Only the white acrylic paint must be opaque.

2 Colour the parts, one side at a time, using a ruler as a mahlstick to steady your brush when painting stripes. Refer to the illustrations for a guide to the colours.
3 The insides of the coats need not be painted, since they will not be seen.

Painting the edges

1 Glue the four coat pieces, fronts and backs, to the two figures, ensuring that they are positioned correctly on the bodies.
2 Paint the edges of the limbs following the surface designs. Paint acrylic white stars on the back of Uncle Sam's blue coat. Paint red, white and blue bars on the back of the coat of the British figure.

Drilling and converting pop-rivets

1 Drill 2mm (0.08in) holes in the bodies, legs, backs and shoulders where indicated. Drill 3mm (0.12in) holes in the hands to allow them to move over the bends in the crankshaft.
2 Pop-rivets, Plan 3, L, need to be converted to make fixings for the limbs. First, with the aid of pliers and a hammer, tap the sliding parts of the rivets until they come loose. Second, remove them from the rivet pins. Keep them for later.
3 Pass each of the four rivet pins through the top of each limb and the bodies so that the pin heads rest on the surfaces.
4 Place the rear facing arms and legs onto the pins.
5 Take the four sliding parts of the rivets which were removed and thread them, inverted now, head first onto the pins.
6 With the inverted heads pushed up against the limbs, ensure that the limbs can move freely before snipping off the ends.
7 It only remains to complete the fixings by dabbing on super-glue (vertically) so that it penetrates the joints.

Gluing and positioning the feet

1 Cut out the feet stabilizers, Plan 2, K. Glue these between each pair of feet.
2 Paint the stabilizers dark blue to match the feet.
3 Glue the feet of the completely jointed figures to the dotted line areas marked on the plinth, Plan 1, B.

Making the paddle block

1 Cut the block from a 20mm (0.79in) square batten (PSE) Plan 3, N, O and P.

The painted figures assembled, with their feet and feet stabilizers glued to the plinth.

Rear view of the figures showing the snipped-off rivet joints in the arms and legs.

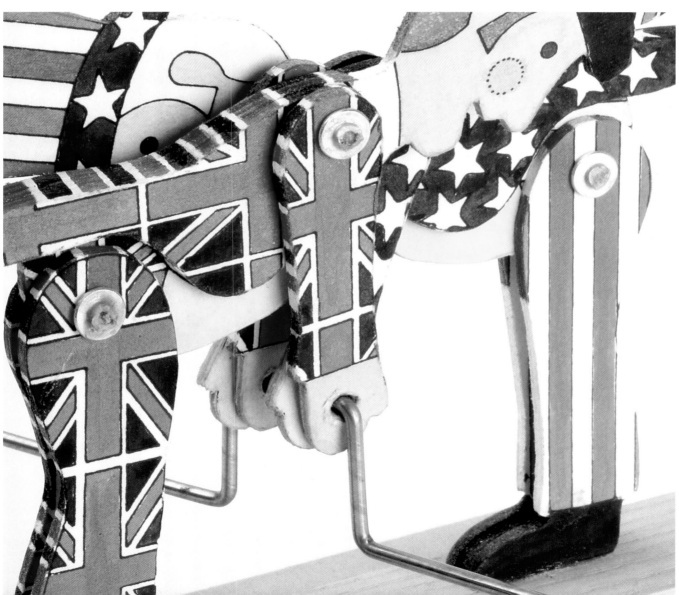

2 Drill a central hole in the block N, to a depth of 17mm (0.67in).

3 Mark off the depths on block O, indicated by the dotted lines.

4 Make four diagonal cuts as shown in the block P, to the indicated depths on block O.

5 Chamfer the edges of the paddle block.

6 File the four slots in the paddle block with a flat needle file so that each paddle, Plan 2 and 3, E and G, fits in snugly up to the dotted line. Place them alternately in the block as shown in the illustrations.

Making the crankshaft and handle

1 With the aid of a vice and hammer, bend the piano wire, Plan 3, K, to the shape on the plan.

2 Cut the dowel handle, Plan 2, L.

3 Cut out the crank from ply, or use stripwood, Plan 2, M. Drill a 6mm (0.24in) hole in one end and a 2mm (0.08) hole in the other end as indicated.

4 Hammer the dowel handle into the larger hole in the crank with glue applied.

5 Cut out the two bearing supports, Plan 2, N. Temporarily bond them together with tape or glue.

Detail of the paddle block showing the central hole for the crankshaft.

Rear view of the paddle block assembly showing the paddles at 45 degrees.

6 Drill a 2.5mm (0.10in) at the top, through the bonded bearing supports.

7 Separate the bearing supports and glue one, as indicated by the dotted rectangle, against the side of the base Plan 1, A, behind the plinth.

Fixing the crankshaft

1 Insert the shorter end of the crankshaft, Plan 3, K, through the 3mm (0.12in) hole in Uncle Sam's right hand.

2 Do likewise with the British figure's left hand, Uncle Sam's left hand and the British figure's right hand, keeping them as close together as possible.

3 Ease the hands, individually, over the 'U' bend in the crankshaft. Squeeze them together so that they are at the bottom of the 'U' shape.

4 Cut out three collets from the dowel rod, Plan 3, M with central holes 2mm (0.08in) drilled in them.

5 Place two of the collets on the crankshaft, so that one goes between the paddle block and rear bearing support and the other, the other side of the rear bearing support.

6 Glue the end of the crankshaft and press it into the paddle block as far as it will go: 17mm (0.67in).

7 Insert the longer end of the crankshaft into the front bearing support, Plan 2, N. It should protrude about 16mm (0.63in).

8 Glue the front bearing support to the front edge of the base, Plan 1, A, opposite the rear bearing support as indicated by the dotted rectangle.

9 Place the third collet, Plan 3, M, onto the end of the crankshaft between the front bearing support and the assembled handle which should be superglued into position.

10 The piece is now ready for clockwise or anti-clockwise operation.

Back view showing the two bearing supports holding the crankshaft and handle before the paddle block is fixed.

The front bearing support, crank handle, collet and crankshaft.

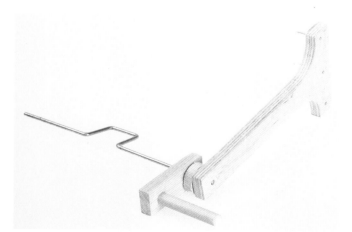

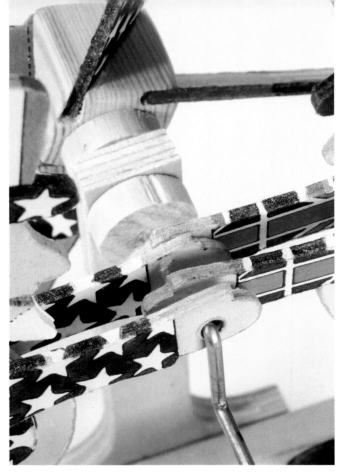

Detail showing disposition of the interleaved hands on the crankshaft. The paddle block is shown with two collets either side of the bearing support.

BELOW LEFT: Detail front view showing the extent of the British figure's nod.

BELOW: Front view of the completed toy.

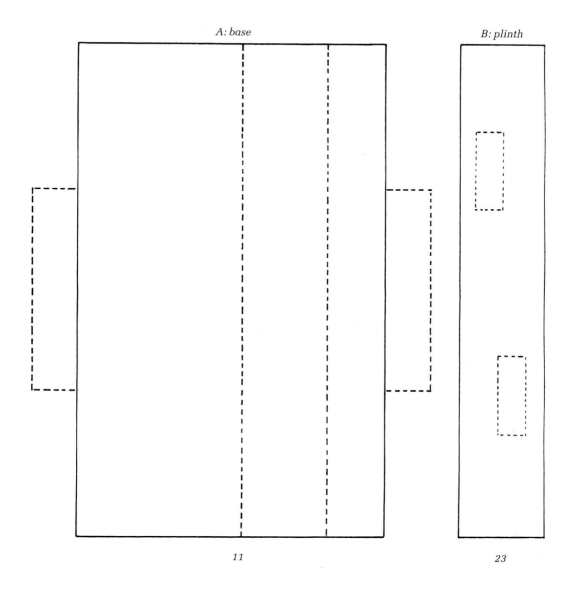

A: base

B: plinth

11

23

Plan 1

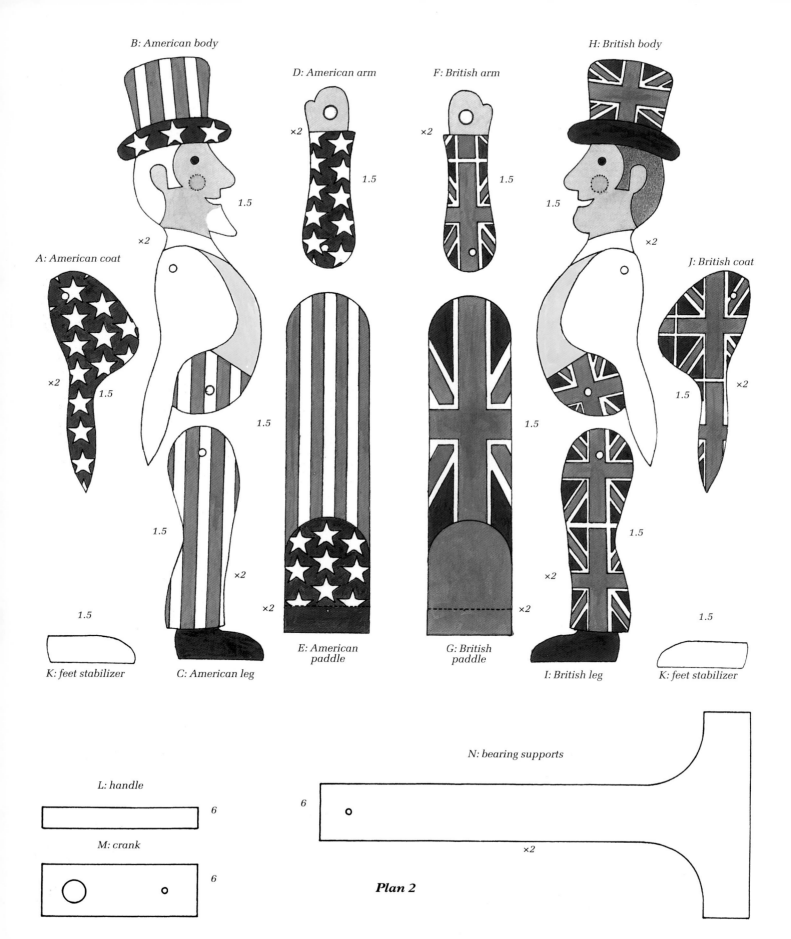

B: American body

D: American arm

×2   1.5

F: British arm

×2   1.5

H: British body

A: American coat

×2

×2   1.5

×2

1.5

J: British coat

×2   1.5

1.5

1.5

1.5

1.5

1.5

×2

×2

×2   1.5

K: feet stabilizer

C: American leg

E: American
paddle

G: British
paddle

I: British leg

K: feet stabilizer

×2

×2

1.5

L: handle   6

N: bearing supports

6

M: crank   6

×2

Plan 2

B: British body

D: British arm
×2
1.5

F: American arm
×2
1.5

H: American body

A: British coat
×2
1.5

×2

O

1.5

J: American coat
1.5
×2

E: British paddle
1.5
1.5
×2
×2

G: American paddle
1.5
×2

C: British leg
1.5
×2

I: American leg
×2
1.5

K: crankshaft

L: pop-rivets

M: 3 collets

N: paddle block hole depth
20

O: paddle block central hole and slot depths
20

P: paddle block diagonal cuts
20

Plan 3

2 CLOTHES-PEG ALLIGATOR

Clothes-pegs come, as a gift, with a ready-made spring mechanism. They cry out to be used as little mechanical toys. The alligator opening and closing its jaws is but one of many ideas which can be harnessed to the simple clothes-peg.

Nodding birds have been used to good effect, for instance, but the mechanism itself should suggest any number of mechanical notions to be brought to life by this extraordinarily efficient little device. Perhaps, with some practice, by synchronizing the action to your voice the alligator can be made to talk!

MATERIALS

AEROPLY	6 × 6 × 1.5mm (0.24 × 0.24 × 0.06in)	Wooden clothes-peg

Cutting out the parts from Aeroply

1 Cut out two birds. These may be cut simultaneously by temporarily bonding two pieces of ply together.
2 Cut the little shelf C, for one bird to stand on.
3 Cut out the reeds D.
4 Cut out the alligator's head E, and lower jaw on the dotted line G, so as to make one cut instead of two.

OPPOSITE: Clothes-peg Alligator.
38 × 102 × 12mm (1.5 × 4.02 × 0.47in).

ABOVE: A household clothes-peg becomes an alligator.

25

Painting the parts

1 Paint one bird looking left and the other looking right.
2 Paint the reeds and their edges dark green.
3 Paint the alligator's head and lower jaw light green, with pink nostrils and white teeth indicated by the dotted line E–F.

Assembling and gluing

1 Glue the head and jaw, interlocked but free of glue, as shown on G, to the clothes-peg.
2 Glue the reeds, resting on the top of the clothes-peg to the back of the head, as shown on E.
3 Stick the little shelf C, to the back of the lower jaw H. Open the clothes-peg to reveal the hidden bird.

RIGHT: A rear view of the surprise in store.

BELOW: The surprise arrives.

BELOW RIGHT: A rear view of the surprise.

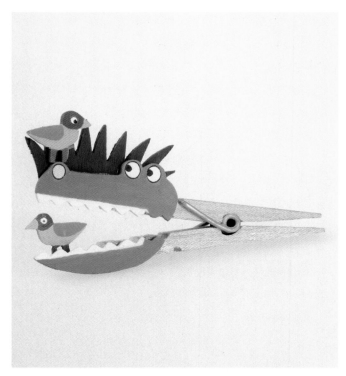

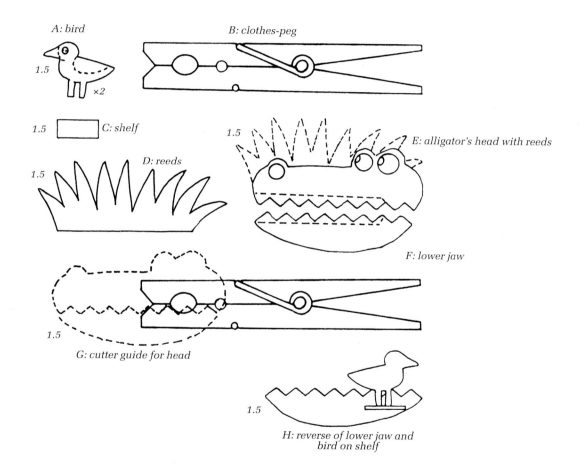

A: bird

1.5

×2

B: clothes-peg

1.5 C: shelf

D: reeds

1.5

1.5 E: alligator's head with reeds

F: lower jaw

G: cutter guide for head

1.5

1.5

H: reverse of lower jaw and bird on shelf

3 AMERICAN SAILBOAT

This toy makes a nod in the direction of that rather special brand of folk-art known as American Country. To qualify, it should be slightly more crudely made, it should not be crisply painted and perhaps it should be ingrained with a little grime. The American author Willa Cather (1873–1947) called it 'that irregular and intimate quality of things made by the human hand'.

The simple mechanism which rocks the boat is provided by an eccentric cam with a circular hole (follower) under the hull of the boat. Two pulleys and an elastic drive band supply the rotary action for the sun. It is a pretty action to watch: the bobbing boat against a spinning sun.

MATERIALS

PLYWOOD	162 × 127 × 5mm (6.38 × 5 × 0.20in)	Sail and sun
DOWEL	30 × 30mm (1.18 × 1.18in)	Four pulley wheels
	16 × 16mm (0.63 × 0.63in)	Two pulley collets
	135 × 6mm (5.32 × 0.24in)	Crankshaft, pulley shaft, handle
SOFTWOOD	220 × 120 × 8mm (8.66 × 4.73 × 0.32in)	Front and back panels
	105 × 90 × 14mm (4.14 × 3.54 × 0.55in)	Boat follower
STRIPWOOD	142 × 12 × 5mm (4.4 × 0.47 × 0.20in)	Support bar, handle
	200 × 20 × 8mm (7.87 × 0.79 × 0.32in)	Two side panels

Cutting out the boat follower and sails from Plan 1

1 Cut out the boat follower A (so-called because it follows the eccentric disc F).
2 Drill, with a hole saw if possible, a central 30mm (1.18in) hole in the boat follower. Keep the disc for later.
3 Cut out the sails I and J, ignoring the dotted line.
4 Take another photocopy of the sails, showing the dotted line. Cut along the dotted line to form the sails stencil cutter guide I–J.

American Sailboat.
203 × 135 × 102mm (8 × 5.32 × 4.02in).

5 Spray-glue the stencil to a sheet of paper for extra strength. Burnish it down firmly and cut out the stars from the reinforced stencil print.
6 Cut out the stripes alternately, starting at the bottom stripe of the sail and continuing to its top little triangle.

Cutting out the sun and sundries from Plan 1

1 Cut out the sun D. Drill a central hole, diameter 6mm (0.24in).
2 Cut out the dowel handle B, and from stripwood cut out the crank C.
3 Cut the pulley collets E from dowel.
4 You will require an eccentric disc F. You may already have a suitable disc if you used a hole saw to cut the hole in the boat follower A. Otherwise, cut a disc from softwood.

The boat follower, including the hull, is cut from one piece of softwood. The sails are stencilled, glued together and fixed to the boat.

5 In either case drill a 6mm (0.24in) hole at the outer edge of the disc as shown on the plan. A central hole appears on the plan which relates to the hole saw and should be ignored.

6 Cut out four top and bottom dowel pulley wheels G and H. Drill central 6mm (0.24in) holes in them.

7 Cut two dowel pulley collets E. Drill central 6mm (0.24in) holes in them.

8 Cut the pulley shaft K from dowel.

9 Cut the crankshaft L from dowel.

10 Cut the support bar for the sun from stripwood.

Cutting out the wave box from Plan 2

1 Temporarily bond two pieces of softwood and cut out the front and back panels using A as a guide. B merely shows the position of the support bar on the reverse of the back panel.

2 Drill a 7mm (0.28in) bearing through the two temporarily bonded panels. Ensure that the crankshaft moves freely within the bearing.

3 Cut out the side panels C from softwood.

Painting the parts from Plans 1 and 2

1 Paint the short stars sail I dark blue on both sides and edges, except the base and vertical edges which are to be glued.

2 Paint the tall stripes sail J white on both sides and edges, except the base and vertical edges.

3 Spray-glue the back of the reinforced sails stencil I–J. Wait until the glue is tacky to the touch (*see* p.11).

4 Carefully place the stencil over the blue sail and press down gently. Only apply just enough pressure to keep it from moving, otherwise it may be difficult to lift up the stencil without damaging the painted surface underneath.

5 Dab white acrylic paint into the stars with a stiff stencil brush. It is better to use too little rather than too much paint in order to avoid paint bleeding under the stencil, and it is useful to experiment before applying the paint. Second and third coats may be needed to achieve full opacity.

6 Repeat the procedure for the white sail. Dab on red acrylic paint with the stencil brush. If paint does bleed under the stencil, it is simple to retouch.

7 Now stencil the backs of the sails exactly as before.

8 Use watered-down blue acrylic colour to stain the front and back panels A and B on Plan 2 and the side panels C so that the attractive grain of the softwood shows through. (Plywood does not have a very pretty grain.)

9 Paint the sun yellow on both sides and also the pulley wheels G and collet E.

10 Paint the lower pulley wheels H and collet E the same blue as used on the wave box.

11 The boat follower and crankshaft remain unpainted.

The sailboat is positioned on the inside of the back panel to receive the crankshaft and eccentric disc. They are inserted through the bearing in the front panel.

Front view of the boat set in the wave box. The end of the support bar for the rotating sun can be seen behind the sails.

Drilling holes in the small parts from Plan 1

1 Drill 6mm (0.24in) holes in the crank C, the two pairs of pulley wheels G and H and the two collets E.
2 Drill a 7mm (0.28in) bearing in the support bar M. Ensure that pulley shaft K turns freely in the support bar bearing.

Assembling the wave box and boat

1 Glue the two sails together along their unpainted edges.
2 Glue their unpainted bottom edges to the deck.
3 Glue both side panels along their edges to the inside of the back panel.
4 Glue the support bar, Plan 1, M, to the back of the back panel as indicated by the dotted line on Plan 2, B.
5 Glue handle B into one of the holes in crank C.
6 Glue crankshaft L into the other hole in the crank.

7 Insert the crankshaft through the front panel.

8 Glue the hole at the edge of the eccentric disc F onto the crankshaft, so that when inserted it is flush with the boat follower. Allow about 3mm (0.12in) between it and the back of the front panel.

9 If you have used a hole saw to cut the eccentric disc F from the boat follower, it will have left a central hole in the disc which should be ignored.

10 Check that the crankshaft and eccentric disc operate smoothly, then glue the front panel to the two side panels. If the boat jams, sand it lightly until it moves freely.

Assembling the sun and pulleys

1 Glue the two upper, yellow, pulley wheels G with their pulley collet E between them.

2 Glue the completed yellow pulley onto the pulley shaft K.

3 Glue the two lower, blue, pulley wheels H with their pulley collet between them.

4 Glue the completed blue pulley onto the protruding end of the crankshaft. But leave a little play so that it is not too tight.

5 Insert the pulley shaft through the 7mm (0.28in) bearing in the support bar.

6 Leaving a little play for easy running between the back of the sun and the support bar, insert and glue the end of the pulley shaft through the central hole in the sun.

7 Fix an elastic band, twisted, to the two pulleys. The twist adds friction to give a more efficient drive. An elastic band of 10mm (0.4in) should be suitable.

8 Turn the crank clockwise, and the sun will rotate anti-clockwise while the boat bobs up and down in the waves.

Rear view showing the support bar for the sun glued in position. The two pulley wheels are shown: one complete with pulley shaft, the other open to show the pulley collet. The last stage is to fix the sun and the drive band.

Rear view of the completed assembly. Twisting the drive band provides extra friction and makes for a smoother movement.

Front view of the finished sailboat which will bob up and down in the waves, while the sun twirls behind.

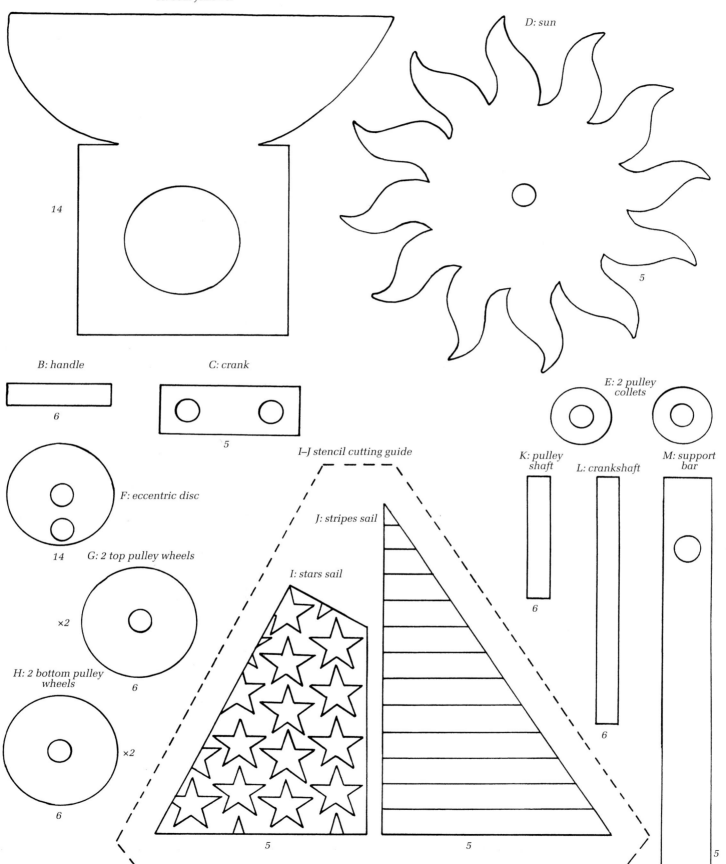

A: boat follower

14

D: sun

5

B: handle

6

C: crank

5

E: 2 pulley collets

I–J stencil cutting guide

K: pulley shaft

L: crankshaft

M: support bar

F: eccentric disc

14

J: stripes sail

G: 2 top pulley wheels

×2

6

I: stars sail

6

H: 2 bottom pulley wheels

×2

6

5

5

6

6

5

Plan 1

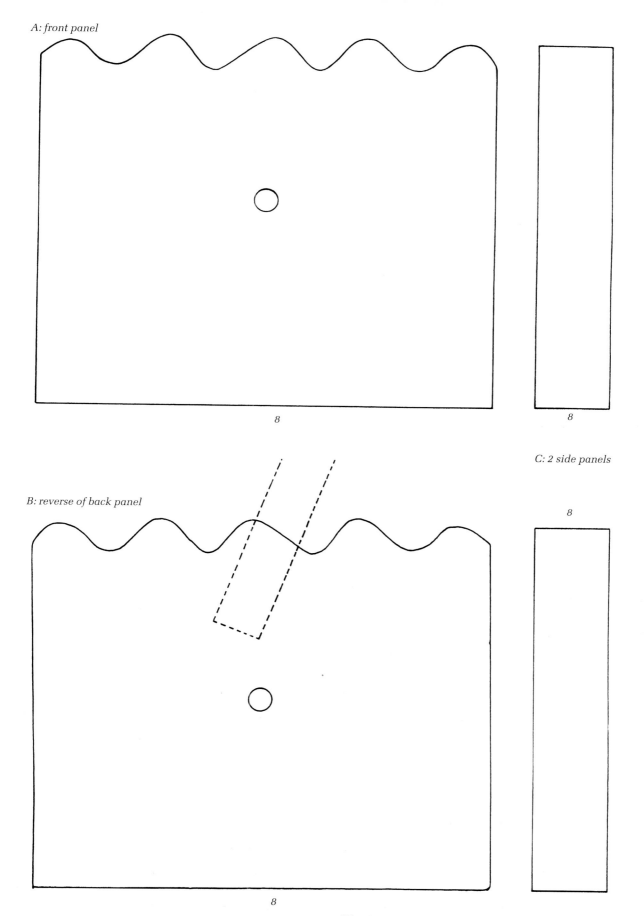

A: front panel

8

8

C: 2 side panels

8

B: reverse of back panel

8

8

Plan 2

4 DRUMMER

The solitary drummer is an easy piece to make and perhaps less daunting than 'A Different Drummer' (*see* Chapter 5) which has four figures to operate and, even more significantly, to paint! The colouring and design are exactly the same (barring the harlequin) for both versions, as is the anti-clockwise mechanism of cam blocks to operate the arms in a drumming motion.

MATERIALS AND EQUIPMENT

PLYWOOD	250 × 200 × 9mm (9.84 × 7.87 × 0.36in)	Box frame, drummer and stand
DOWEL	80 × 16mm (3.15 × 0.63) 160 × 6mm (6.3 × 0.24in)	Drum, collets Camshaft, handle
BATTENING (PSE)	40 × 14 × 14mm (1.58 × 0.55 × 0.55in)	Cam blocks
STRIPWOOD	70 × 20 × 6mm (2.76 × 0.79 × 0.24in) 40 × 14 × 6mm (1.58 × 0.55 × 0.24in)	Arms Crank

Two screw eyes
Two pop rivets

Cutting the drummer from the plan

1 Cut out the drummer H using a photocopy of the design spray-glued onto plywood.
2 Keep the surface design when you peel it off the figure, because it will be needed in order to transfer the design onto the drummer. If it is damaged, an extra photocopy may be needed.
3 Temporarily bond two pieces of stripwood and cut out two arms G.
4 Cut out the stand N from plywood.

Drilling holes in the figure and arms

1 Drill a 1mm (0.04in) hole in both shoulders of the drummer as indicated on H.
2 Drill 1.5mm (0.06in) holes in the temporarily bonded upper arms G where indicated. All holes will have to

Drummer. 148 × 133 × 73mm (5.83 × 5.24 × 2.87in).

be re-drilled once the figure is painted, but they are positioned at this stage.
3 Drill 2.5mm (0.10in) holes in the hands.
4 Holding the arms in a vice, carefully drill 1.5mm (0.06in) holes in the back of each arm as indicated by the dotted line on G.
5 Now, carefully screw the screw eyes L into the top edge of each arm. There is a danger that the wood will split, but since the arms are held in a vice, this should not happen.
6 Separate the arms and sand them with chamfered edges.

Making the castellated frame from plywood

1 Cut the base A from the plan.
2 Cut out the two side panels F and temporarily bond them with tape.
3 Drill a 7mm (0.28in) hole through both panels. This is the bearing for the camshaft.

4 Draw a pencil line across the bottom edges of the panels so that you can tell, when they have been separated, which way round they should be assembled. Once they have been marked, they can be separated.

5 Cut out the castellated architrave C and its two supports M.

6 Glue them together, at the ends, as shown in the illustrations.

Making the camshaft
1 Cut the dowel handle P.
2 Cut the crank Q from stripwood.
3 Drill two 6mm (0.24in) holes in the crank.
4 Glue and tap the dowel handle into the crank.
5 Now fix the other hole in the crank onto the camshaft B.
6 Cut dowel collets I and J and glue one up against the crank handle.
7 Cut the dowel B. This is the camshaft, and the divisions for positioning the cams are marked on the plan.
8 Lightly spray-glue a photocopy of the shaft and stick it to the dowel rod. Prick on each dotted line to mark the intervals.
9 Cut the two cam blocks E from softwood. Drill central holes in them, 6mm (0.24in).
10 Slide the two cam blocks, tightly fitting, onto the camshaft in their positions for fixing, but do not glue.
11 The other collet J is used as an end stop and should be fitted (but not glued) at this stage. When the piece is fully assembled, it will appear (painted) on the outer side of the left-hand side panel.

Camshaft with handle and collet and two cam blocks.

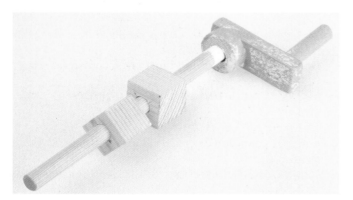

Priming the drummer
1 Prime the fronts and sides of the figure with matt white emulsion, or vinyl matt white emulsion if you are using acrylic paint. Apply a second coat if necessary.
2 Prime the arms, except for the screw eyes, white all over.
3 Prime the drums white.
4 Sand all pieces when dry.

Painting the drummer
1 Transfer the designs from the plan to the primed and sanded white figure and arms. Refer to the notes on painting and transferring designs (*see* pp 10–11).
2 Paint the drummer and arms, referring to the plans and illustrations. Paint the back of the figure green, together with its support N.
3 Paint the drum design using K as a guide. To help with painting, drill a 1mm (0.04in) hole in the base of the drum to a depth of 10mm (0.4in). Insert a panel pin into the hole and press the head into an empty toilet roll tube or a lump of modelling clay in order to keep the drum steady for painting.
4. Sand off a vertical strip from the back of the drum to allow it to be glued to the figure.

Fixing arms, drum and drumsticks
1 Select two household pins with good heads on them, and cut them to 10mm (0.4in). For safety, insert the pins into modelling clay or similar so that the sharp ends are held safely when snipped off, and dispose of the pointed ends carefully.
2 Insert the pins through the painted arms into the shoulder blades of the figures which are super-glued to receive the pins. Ensure that the arms move freely.
3 Snip off the ends of two pop rivets O to make drumsticks and file off the ends.
4 Now, insert the two snipped off pop-rivet drumsticks half way into the hands. There should be some play in the holes so that the drumsticks can be superglued at an angle to the body. Fill the residue with modelling putty. Paint the drumsticks white.
5 Place the painted drum, at an angle, so that the slightly inward facing drumstick heads are over the centre of the drum. Test the drumming action and then glue them in position so that the drumsticks strike the drum when the arms move.

Priming the castellated box frame

1 Prime the base A and its outer edges (except the back) with matt white (vinyl) emulsion.
2 Prime the side panels F on both sides, front and top edges, white.
3 Prime the back panel on its front and two side edges, white.
4 Prime the castellated architrave, with its supports, white on its front, back and side edges.
5 Prime the collets J (the end stop) and I (glued to the handle), white.

Painting the castellated box frame

1 Using a dry sponge approximately 50mm (2in) square and acrylic or stencil paint, dab light grey paint onto the back and side panels where they are painted white. Try to achieve a stone effect, leaving bits of white showing through. Finish off with a paint brush.
2 Do the same for the castellated architrave and the collets and handle assembly.
3 Paint the white parts of the base green. Two coats will be required.
4 Cut out a stencil of the anti-clockwise arrow on the side panel F.
5 Lightly spray-glue the back of the stencil and position it above the bearing as indicated on F. Use a stencil brush dipped in red paint to stencil the design onto the panel.

The castellated architrave on top of the side panel showing the stencilled arrow for anti-clockwise hand cranking.

Assembling the camshaft and box frame

1 Insert the camshaft through the bearing on the inside of panel F, with the stencilled arrow.
2 Glue the painted collet and handle to the end of the camshaft.
3 Insert the camshaft, with the cams in position, through the bearing in the other side panel F.
4 Glue the painted collet end stop J to the end of the projecting camshaft.
5 Holding the camshaft, glue and pin the side panels to the base as indicated on the plan.
6 Glue and pin the back panel D, as indicated in the plan, to the back edges of the side panels.
7 Glue the painted architrave to the forward tops of the side panels to make the box rigid. Tap in panel pins into the centre of the supports.

Rear view of drummer and stand.

Positioning the cams and drummer

1 Glue the stand N to the back of the drummer's legs.
2 Twist the cams on the shaft so that the left cam faces square on and the right cam points upwards like a diamond.
3 Place the drummer against the cams and ensure that the arms are operating correctly, winding anti-clockwise. Mark around the feet faintly in pencil.
4 Now, superglue the 'T' shape of the stand and feet into the position you marked in pencil.
5 Wind the piece anti-clockwise only. Check that the cams are engaging with the screw eyes at the back of the arms.
6 Once satisfied with the action, apply superglue to either side of each cam, all the way round.

The complete piece showing the collet end stop glued to the end of the camshaft.

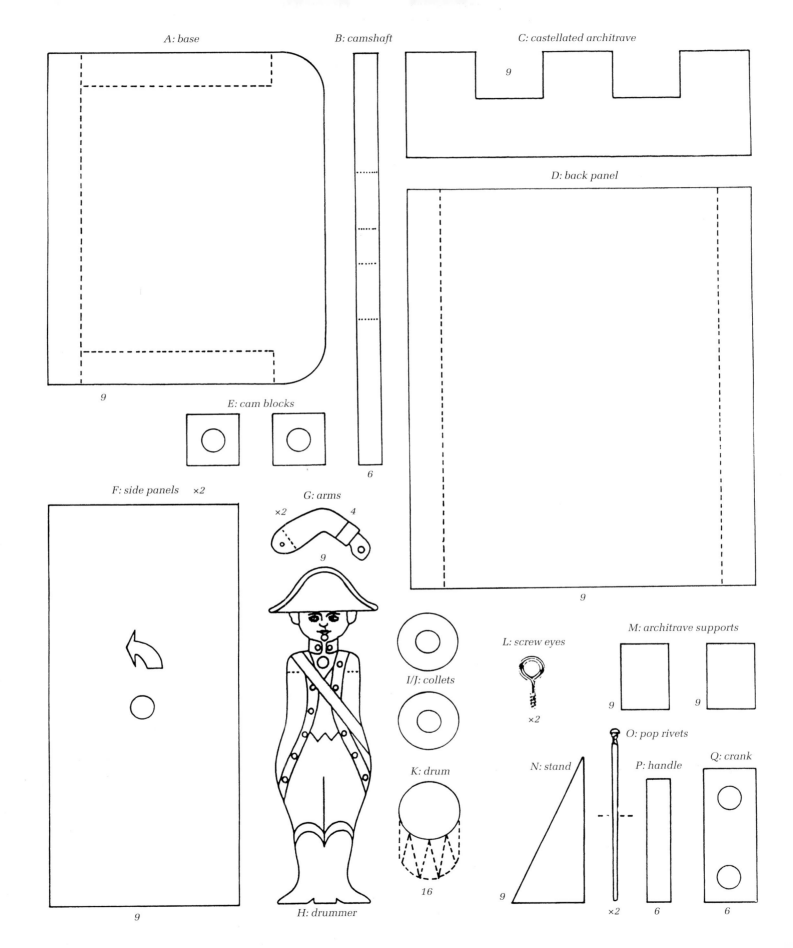

A: base

B: camshaft

C: castellated architrave

9

D: back panel

9

9

9

E: cam blocks

6

F: side panels ×2

G: arms

×2 4

9

9

I/J: collets

L: screw eyes

M: architrave supports

×2

9 9

K: drum

O: pop rivets

N: stand

P: handle

Q: crank

16

9

×2

6

6

H: drummer

5 A DIFFERENT DRUMMER

This is a companion piece to 'The Bluebelles' (*see* Chapter 15) which also features someone out of step with their fellows. Here, the harlequin drums a different rhythm to the other drummers. Henry David Thoreau (1817–62) had this to say:

If a man does not keep pace with his companions, perhaps it is because he hears a different drummer. Let him step to the music he hears, however measured or far away.

A simple series of cam blocks operate the arms, which have screw eyes attached to them acting as levers. The piece can only be turned anti-clockwise.

MATERIALS

PLYWOOD	250 × 400 × 9mm (9.84 × 15.75 × 0.36in)	Box frame, figures
DOWEL	80 × 16mm (3.15 × 0.63in)	Four drums, two collets
	300 × 6mm (11.81 × 0.24in)	Camshaft, handle
BATTENING (PSE)	120 × 14 × 14mm (4.73 × 0.55 × 0.55in)	Cam blocks
STRIPWOOD	240 × 20 × 6mm (9.45 × 0.79 × 0.24in)	Arms
	40 × 14 × 6mm (1.58 × 0.55 × 0.24in)	Crank

Eight screw eyes
Eight pop rivets

Cutting out the figures from Plan 1

1 Using a photocopy spray-glued onto a piece of plywood as a guide, cut out two figures each from C and F. They are all the same shape so if you temporarily bond two pieces of plywood together, you can cut a soldier and the harlequin simultaneously.
2 After cutting the figures, carefully remove the photocopies and put them to one side, as you will need them in order to transfer the designs to the figures.
3 Cut four pairs of arms B and E from stripwood. Again, don't worry about the harlequin's differently designed arms as they are all the same shape. They can be cut four together, if you drill small holes as register marks outside the arms. If you decide to do this, dab a little glue on each hole to hold the pieces together temporarily.
4 From Plan 2, cut four stands D from plywood by temporarily bonding two pieces together and cutting two at a time.
5 Cut the diagonal and release the four triangular stands.

Drilling holes in the figures and arms

1 With the parts still held together, drill 1mm (0.04in) holes in both shoulders of the figures C and F. That is eight holes in total, the depths indicated by the dotted lines.

A Different Drummer.
148 × 280 × 73mm (5.82 × 1.10 × 2.87in).

2 Drill 1.5mm (0.06in) holes in the temporarily bonded upper arms B and E where indicated. All these holes will have to be redrilled once the figures are painted, but they are positioned at this stage.

3 Drill 2.5mm (0.10in) holes in the hands of these arms B and E.

4 Holding the arms in a vice, carefully drill 1.5mm (0.06in) holes in the back of each arm as indicated by the dotted lines on B, under each arm hole.

5 Now, carefully screw the screw eyes D into the top edge of each arm. There is a danger that the wood will split, but since the arms are held in a vice, this should not happen.

6 Dismantle all the pieces which have been temporarily bonded together and sand them off with chamfered edges.

Making the castellated box frame from plywood

1 Cut out the base A from Plan 2.

2 Cut out the two side panels J from Plan 2 and temporarily bond them together with tape.

3 Drill a 7mm (0.28in) hole through them to create the bearing for the camshaft.

4 Draw a pencil line across the bottom edges of the panels so that when they have been separated, it will be possible to tell which way they should be assembled. You can separate them now they have been marked.

5 Cut out the castellated architrave A from Plan 1 and its two supports C on Plan 2.

6 Glue them together, at the ends, as shown in the illustration.

Making the camshaft from Plan 2

1 Cut the dowel handle G.

2 Cut the crank I from stripwood.

3 Drill two 6mm (0.24in) holes in the crank.

4 Glue and tap the dowel handle into the crank.

5 Now fix the camshaft F into the hole in the crank handle.

6 Cut dowel collets E and glue one up against the crank handle.

7 Cut the dowel F. This is the camshaft and the divisions for positioning the cams are marked on the plan.

8 Lightly spray-glue a photocopy of the shaft and stick it to the dowel rod. Prick on each dotted line to mark off the intervals.

9 Cut the eight cam blocks H from softwood. Drill central holes in them, 6mm (0.24in).

10 If the blocks are too tight to fit on the dowel rod they may need to be widened very slightly by the drill or by filing.

11 Slide the cam blocks, tightly fitting, onto the camshaft, roughly in their final position for fixing.

12 The other collet E is used as an end-stop and should be fitted (but not glued) at this stage. When the piece is fully assembled it will appear (painted) on the outer side of the left-hand side panel.

Priming the figures and drums

1 Prime the fronts and sides of the figures with matt white emulsion or vinyl matt emulsion if you are using acrylic paint. Apply a second coat, if necessary.

2 Prime the arms entirely white.

3 Prime the drums white, as you did with the figures and arms.

4 Sand all pieces when dry.

Camshaft held within its side panel bearings.

Painting the figures and drums

1 Transfer the design from the plan to the painted and sanded white figures and arms. Refer to the notes on painting and transferring designs (*see* pp10–11).

2 Paint the figures and arms by referring to the plans and illustrations. Paint the backs of the figures green, together with their four supports.

3 Paint the drums using B on Plan 2 as a guide. To help with painting, drill a 1mm (0.04in) hole in the base of each drum to a depth of 10mm (0.4in). Insert panel pins into the holes and press their heads into an empty toilet roll tube or a lump of modelling clay in order to keep the drums steady for painting.

4 Sand off a vertical strip at the back of each drum, enough to allow them to be glued to the figures.

Fixing arms, drums and drumsticks

1 Cut eight household pins, with good heads on them, to 10mm (0.4in). For safety, insert the sharp ends of the pins into modelling clay before snipping them off, so that they are held safely. When disposing of the pointed ends, make sure that they are wrapped safely.

2 Insert the pins, through the painted arms, into the shoulder blades of the figures which are superglued to receive the pins. Ensure that the arms move freely.

3 Snip the ends off the eight pop rivets to form drumsticks K as indicated on Plan 2. File off the cut ends.

4 Now, insert the eight snipped-off pop-rivet drumsticks half way into four pairs of hands. There should be some play in the holes so that the drumsticks can be superglued at an angle to the bodies. Fill the residue with modelling putty or plastic wood. Paint the drumsticks white.

5 Place the painted drums, at an angle, so that the drumstick heads are over the centre of the drums. Glue them in position so that the drumsticks will strike the drums when the arms move.

Priming the castellated box frame

1 All of the pieces listed below should be primed by painting with matt white (vinyl) emulsion.

2 Paint the base A on Plan 2 and its outer edges (except the back).

3 Paint both sides and the front and top edges of the side panels J.

4 Paint the front and two side edges of the back panel.

5 Paint the front, back and side edges of the castellated architrave and its supports.

6 Paint the collets (the end stop and the one glued to the handle).

Painting the castellated box frame

1 Using a dry sponge approximately 50mm (2in) square and acrylic or stencil paint, dab light grey paint onto the back and side panels where they are painted white. Try to achieve a stone effect, leaving bits of white showing through. Finish off with a paint-brush.

2 Do the same for the castellated architrave and the collets and handle assembly.

3 Where the base has been primed with white paint, it should now be painted green. Two coats will be required.

4 Cut out a stencil of the anti-clockwise arrow on the side panel J on Plan 2.

5 Lightly spray-glue the back of the stencil and position it above the bearing, as indicated on J. Use a stencil brush dipped in red paint to stencil the design onto the panel.

Castellated architrave with supports.

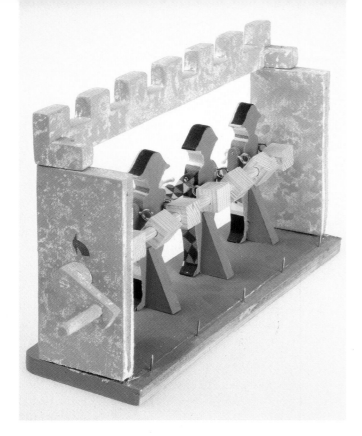

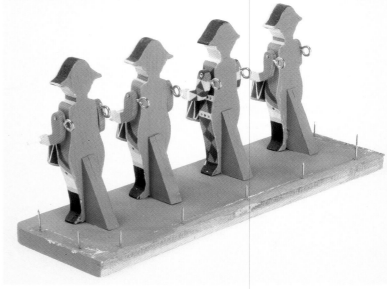

LEFT: *Rear view of castellated box frame with back panel removed.*

ABOVE: *Rear view of the supported figures showing the series of screw eyes acting as levers for the cams.*

BELOW: *Bird's eye view showing positioning of alternately placed cam blocks.*

BELOW RIGHT: *Detail front view of the figures. Harlequin is out of time.*

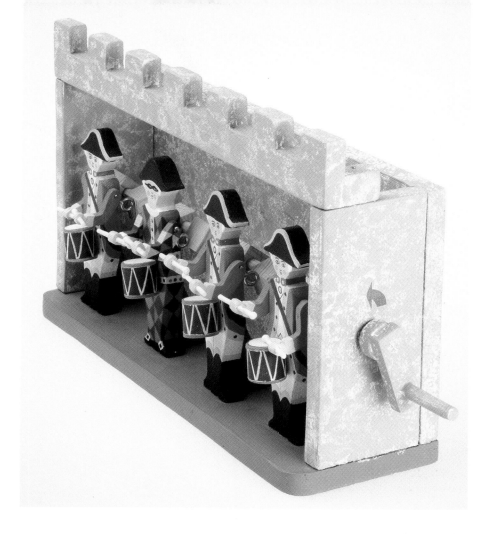

The completed piece showing the anti-clockwise arrow above the crank handle.

Assembling the camshaft and box frame

1 Insert the camshaft through the bearing on the inside of panel J (onto which the arrow has been stencilled).
2 Glue the painted collet and handle to the end of the camshaft.
3 Insert the camshaft with the cams in their, approximate, temporary positions through the bearing in the other side panel J.
4 Glue the painted collet end stop E to the end of the projecting camshaft.
5 Glue and pin the side panels, holding the camshaft, to the base as indicated on Plan 2, A.
6 Glue and pin the back panel G, as indicated on Plan 2, to the back edges of the side panels.
7 Glue the painted architrave to the forward tops of the side panels to make the box rigid. Tap in panel pins into the centre of the supports.

Positioning the cams and figures

1 Glue the four stands D on Plan 2 to the back of each figure's legs.
2 Twist the soldiers' cams on the shaft so their left cams face square on and their right cams point upwards, like diamonds.
3 Twist the harlequin's left cam into a diamond and his right cam into a square. This enables him to drum out of time with his companions.
4 Place each figure against its two corresponding cams and ensure that the arms are operating correctly, winding anti-clockwise. Mark around the feet faintly in pencil.
5 Superglue the 'T' shape of the stand and feet into the positions you marked in pencil.
6 Wind the piece anti-clockwise only. Check that all the cams are engaging with the screw eyes at the back of the arms.
7 Once satisfied with the action, apply superglue to either side of each cam, all the way round.

A: castellated architrave   B: soldier's arms   G: back panel

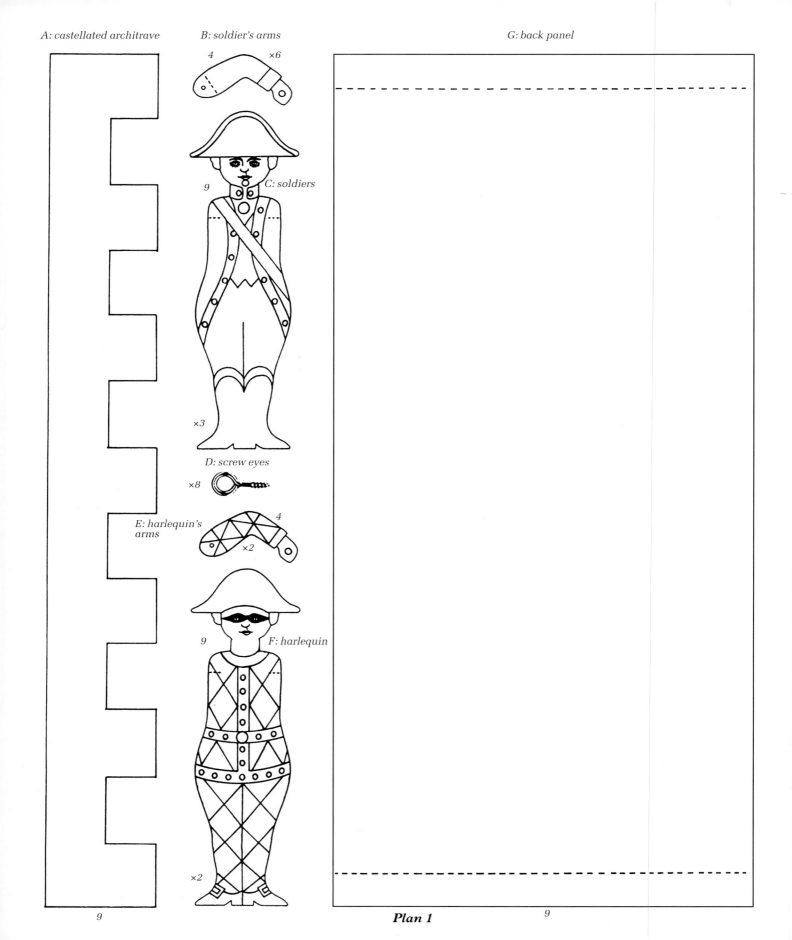

4   ×6

C: soldiers

9

×3

D: screw eyes

×8

E: harlequin's
arms

4

×2

F: harlequin

9

×2

9   **Plan 1**   9

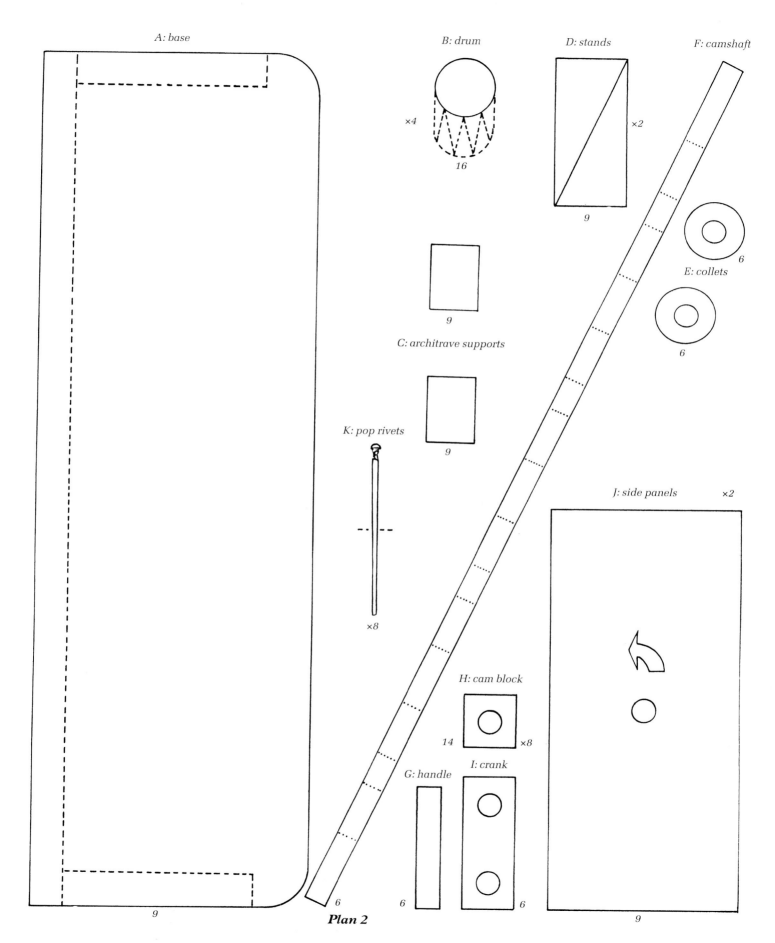

A: base

B: drum

D: stands

F: camshaft

×4

16

×2

9

E: collets

6

6

C: architrave supports

9

9

K: pop rivets

J: side panels   ×2

×8

H: cam block

14   ×8

G: handle   *I: crank*

6   6   6

Plan 2

9   9

6 KINETIC CRYSTALS

The piece is held in one hand and operated by the other, either clockwise or anti-clockwise, setting up an attractive kinetic whirring display: slow at the front; fast at the back. Magic! I am not aware of any other similar toys, but I would be pleased to hear of any examples.

The four crystals have been designed in such a way so as to make each element easily visible. By twisting alternate driving belts the crystal discs are made to turn in opposite directions to each other. It makes an attractive, geometrical, shelf-piece.

MATERIALS

PLYWOOD	330 × 30 × 9mm (13 × 13 × 0.36in)	Box
	400 × 350 × 3mm (15.75 × 13.78 × 0.12in)	Crystal discs
STRIPWOOD	60 × 20 × 5mm (2.36 × 0.79 × 0.20in)	Crank
DOWEL	150 × 12mm (5.9 × 0.47in)	Drive shaft, handle
	110 × 6mm (4.34 × 0.24in)	Pulley shaft
	70 × 25mm (2.76 × 0.98in)	Collets
	50 × 8mm (1.97 × 0.32in)	Arbors
BATTENING (PSE)	50 × 23 × 23mm (1.97 × 0.91 × 0.91in)	Bearing extensions

Four (Mamod) flexible steel spring driving belts 350 × 2mm (13.78 × 0.08in), to be cut to length.

Cutting the crystal discs and pulley arbors

1 You will require four photocopies of Plan 1 in order to cut each crystal A, B, C and D.
2 From the photocopies, cut out each crystal roughly and spray-glue the backs.
3 Stick the four prints to plywood.
4 Cut out the crystal discs from plywood.
5 Drill 12mm (0.47in) central holes in each disc.
6 Cut four pulley wheel arbors G from dowel.
7 Tap and glue each arbor, with a tight friction fit, into the crystal discs. They will protrude 4mm (0.16in) above the surface of the discs.

Kinetic Crystals.
278 × 178 × 152mm (10.95 × 7.01 × 5.98in).

8 Drill 7mm (0.28in) holes in the centre of each arbor.

Fixing the crystal discs onto the pulley shaft

1 Cut the pulley shaft B on Plan 2 from dowel.
2 Cut four pulley shaft collets I from 25mm (0.98in) dowel.
3 Drill central 7mm (0.28) holes in the collets so that each crystal can spin freely on the pulley shaft.
4 Cut two pulley shaft collet stops M from dowel.
5 Drill central 6mm (0.24in) holes in them.
6 Glue one collet stop to the end of the pulley shaft. (The other will fit onto the shaft, inside the box, later.)
7 Glue the protruding arbors G to the pulley collets I to make pulley wheels.

8   Roughen the pulley channels with a saw to improve the grip for the drive bands.

Making the box from 9mm (0.36in) plywood

1   Cut out the front panel A on Plan 3.
2   Drill a 12mm (0.47in) hole in the lower part of the front panel, as indicated. This will need to be widened slightly to allow the 12mm (0.47in) dowel shaft to move freely within its bearing, but this should be done after painting.

Detail showing crystal discs and embedded arbor. These are drilled to take the rotating shaft and stuck to a collet to make a pulley.

3   Drill a 7mm (0.28in) hole in the upper part of the front panel, as indicated.
4   Cut out the two side panels D from Plan 2, together if possible.
5   Cut out the two end panels C, together if possible. These will be the top and base since it is a vertical piece.
6   If you have spray-glued photocopies of the designs onto the plywood, do not discard the star designs after you have removed them. They will serve as stencil cutting guides when you paint the box.
7   Glue and pin the box together as instructed in the general notes (*see* p.11). The dotted lines indicate positioning.

Making the handle and drive shaft

1   Cut the drive shaft A on Plan 2, from dowel.
2   Cut the four drive shaft collets H from dowel.
3   Drill 12mm (0.47in) holes in their centres.
4   Cut the handle E from dowel.
5   Cut the crank F from stripwood. Drill 12mm (0.47in) holes as indicated.
6   Cut the two drive shaft collet stops L. Drill 12mm (0.47in) holes in their centres.
7   Cut the two bearing extensions, J for the pulley shaft and K for the drive shaft, from 23mm (0.91in) square battening (PSE).
8   Drill central holes in them, 7mm (0.28in) in J and 12mm (0.47in) in K, as indicated. The latter will need to be widened, enough to accommodate the drive shaft turning freely.

Painting and stencilling

1   Prime and paint the box and all parts except for those inside the box and the two shafts. Refer to the general notes on painting and stencilling (*see* p.11).
2   To make the star stencils from Plan 2, C and D, either use the designs which you peeled off the side panels or make a new photocopy.
3   In either event the photocopies will need to be reinforced to make a satisfactory stencil. Spray-glue the star designs onto paper and burnish them down firmly.
4   With the aid of a steel rule, cut out the stars from their panels.
5   Lightly spray-glue the back of one of the stencils and position it on a side panel.
6   Using silver (acrylic) paint, dab a stencil brush into the stencil. Two applications should be sufficient to cover the dark blue ground. Work sparingly.

7 When dry, lift off the stencil and repeat the process for the other side and the end panels.

Assembling the handle and drive shaft

1 Tap and glue the handle E on Plan 2 into one of the holes in the crank F, with a tight friction fit.
2 Tap and glue the drive shaft A into the other hole in the crank.
3 Slide a drive shaft collet H onto the drive shaft A and glue it in position against the crank F.
4 Glue the other three collets onto the drive shaft leaving 3mm (0.12in) gaps between each.
5 Glue one of the drive shaft collet stops L last on the shaft.
6 Insert the drive shaft into the slightly enlarged 12mm (0.47in) lower hole in the front panel. Ensure that the shaft still moves freely in the bearing after it has been painted.
7 Insert the end of the drive shaft through the bearing extension K and glue the extension to the inside of the box. Ensure that the shaft moves freely within its extended bearing.
8 Glue the other collet stop L onto the drive shaft almost up to the bearing extension, not too tight, to allow enough play for the shaft to turn freely in its bearing.

Crank handle and drive shaft with four collets and end stop. The unpainted end stop is fixed to the shaft inside the box.

Assembling the crystal discs

1 Cut four flexible steel driving belts 300mm × 2mm (11.81in × 0.08in) and join the ends, twisting them into each other anti-clockwise (left-hand thread).
2 Hold the pulley shaft B on Plan 2, which has an end stop M glued to the end, and slide on the smallest (light blue) disc.
3 Put the discs on the pulley shaft in ascending order of size, hanging a joined driving belt from each pulley.
4 Insert the pulley shaft with the assembled discs through the upper hole in the front panel of the box.

Inside the box you can see the upper and lower bearing extensions and the collet stops.

5 Glue the pulley shaft extension J to the inside of the box, ensuring that the shaft turns freely in its 7mm (0.28in) bearing.

6 Glue the other pulley shaft collet stop M onto the pulley shaft, allowing sufficient play between it and the bearing extension J. Ensure that the shaft can turn freely in its extended bearing.

Arranging the driving belts

1 Make a twist in the driving belt of the largest disc, at the back. Pull it over the handle and around the drive shaft, between the silver collet and the dark blue end stop.

2 The next belt, hanging between the silver and dark blue discs, goes between the silver and dark blue collets on the drive shaft, without a twist.

3 Twist the next belt, between the yellow and dark blue discs and put it around its corresponding collets on the drive shaft.

4 The last belt goes around the drive shaft between the yellow and light blue collets.

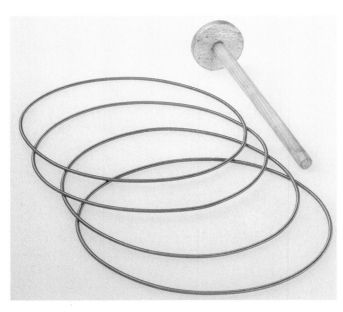

Four flexible steel driving belts and the pulley shaft with end stop.

The crystal discs assembled on the pulley shaft with their driving belts between them and the collets.

The pulley shaft, with its end stop, is inserted into four discs with driving belts in between each.

The driving belts, ready to be fixed to the drive shaft, will be twisted to provide backward rotation and placed straight to go forwards.

5 When all the pulleys have been arranged in order, the Kinetic Crystal can be made to perform. Holding the piece upright in one hand and winding the handle with the other, the discs rotate in opposite directions: slow at the front and fast at the back.

The completed assembly shows alternately twisted and straight driving belts which give backward and forward rotation.

A: front panel

A: silver crystal; B: dark blue crystal; C: yellow crystal; D: light blue crystal
(note that these should be cut 3mm (0.12in) thick from four photocopies).

Plan 1

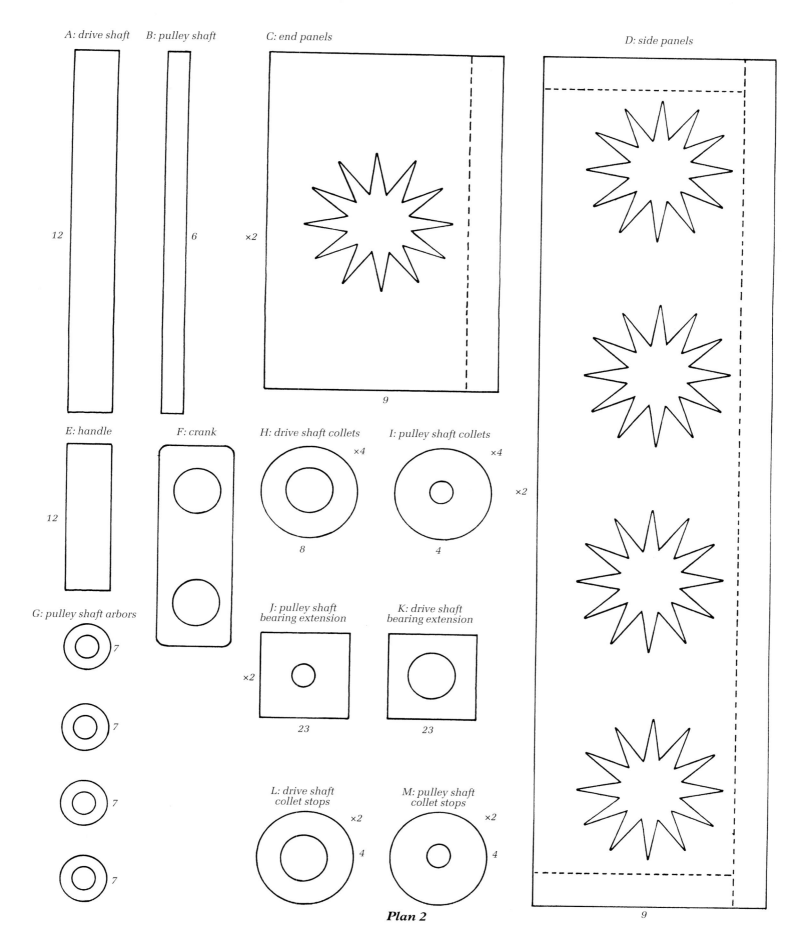

Plan 2

7 LOVE DOVES

This piece shows an open mechanism which is almost as interesting to watch as the intimate behaviour of the doves. Mechanisms are not often painted since they are usually hidden from view, and also because after painting they can be a bit sticky to operate. However if painted thinly, almost stained, they should function adequately when sanded down.

Turning the camshaft, with the outer eccentric cam discs pointing up and the inner ones down (or vice versa) causes the disc followers with the hearts to move apart, together and up and down. So the birds do a little hop as they kiss in a series of little pecks. It is quite easy to construct and makes an ideal three-dimensional Valentine's card.

MATERIALS

PLYWOOD	250 × 300 × 9mm (9.84 × 11.81 × 0.36in)	Box frame, doves
	140 × 100 × 5mm (5.5 × 3.94 × 0.20in)	Wings
DOWEL	60 × 36mm (2.36 × 1.42in)	Disc followers
	50 × 28mm (1.97 × 1.10in)	Cams
	50 × 15mm (1.97 × 0.59in)	Collets
	400 × 6mm (15.75 × 0.24in)	Camshaft and shafts, handle
	120 × 3mm (4.72 × 0.12in)	Follower rods
STRIPWOOD	160 × 45 × 4mm (6.3 × 1.77 × 0.16in)	Hearts, hearts panel
	50 × 20 × 6mm (1.97 × 0.79 × 0.24in)	Crank

Making the box frame

1 Cut out the top and base panels D on Plan 2. If possible, cut both panels simultaneously by temporarily bonding two piece of plywood together. After cutting, separate the two panels.
2 Drill 7mm (0.28in) holes in the top panel only, as shown.
3 Cut the side panels H, again cutting both panels simultaneously by temporarily bonding two pieces of plywood.
4 Drill a central 7mm (0.28in) hole through both panels before separating them.
5 Glue and pin the sides H to the top and base panels D, referring to the diagram on Plan 1. Refer to the instructions for making boxes (see pp12–13).

Love Doves.
197 × 178 × 108mm (7.75 × 7.01 × 4.26in).

Making the camshaft and handle

1 Cut the camshaft C on Plan 2 from dowel.
2 Cut the handle G from dowel.
3 Cut the crank L from stripwood.
4 Drill two holes in the crank as indicated.
5 Cut the collets J and K from dowel.
6 Drill central 6mm (0.24in) holes in the collets.
7 Cut four eccentric discs, Plan 2, A from dowel.
8 Drill eccentric holes in them, as marked on the plan.

Making the disc followers, shafts and platform

1 Cut two disc followers, Plan 3, A from dowel, or from plywood if dowel is unavailable.
2 Drill central 6mm (0.24in) holes in the followers.
3 Drill 3mm (0.12in) lateral holes in the followers' sides, as indicated on Plan 3, A.
4 Cut the follower rods E from dowel.

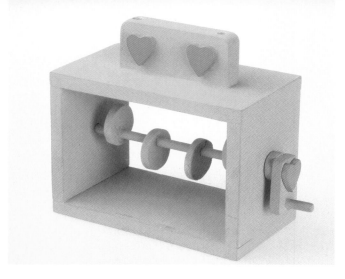

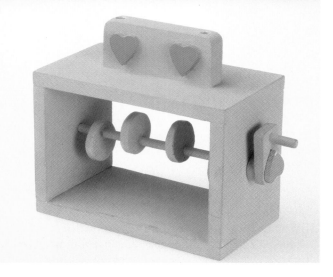

The box frame and platform with eccentric cams on the ends of the camshaft facing up and, in the centre, facing down, as is the handle.

The box frame and platform with the eccentric cams on the ends of the camshaft facing down and, in the centre, facing up, as is the handle.

5   Cut the two shafts G from dowel.
6   Cut the platform B on Plan 2 from plywood.
7   Drill 7mm (0.28in) holes, vertically, either end, as shown in the diagram on Plan 2.
8   Cut out the platform hearts E on Plan 2, from strip-wood.

9   Cut out the crank heart I from stripwood, as above.
10   Glue the platform B to the top D, over the holes, within the dotted line area, so that the holes match.
11   Test the shafts in the holes in the platform and top so that they move freely.

The doves with shafts inserted (but not glued). Between them, above, is the hearts panel. This acts as a stop to the follower rods attached to the hearts.

Cutting out the doves from Plan 3

1 From plywood, cut out the two doves D. If possible, temporarily bond two pieces together so that both doves can be cut simultaneously. Otherwise dove B, the painting guide, can serve as a cutting guide. Remember that you will need to refer to the design when painting, so make an extra photocopy if necessary.

2 Drill 6mm (0.24in) holes in the doves, as indicated by the dotted line of the shafts. It is important to get the correct angle and depth or the doves' beaks won't meet when performing and their tails may scrape the ground.

3 Tap the shafts G, with a tight friction-fit, into the doves. Don't glue in case you need to adjust the lengths.

4 Cut out, together, two pairs of wings F from plywood.

5 Glue the wings to either side of the doves as shown by the dotted line.

6 Cut out the two follower hearts C together from strip-wood, but don't separate them.

7 Drill 4mm (0.12in) holes in the hearts, as indicated, and then separate them.

8 Tap and glue the follower rods E into the follower hearts with a tight friction fit.

Priming and painting the parts

1 Prime all parts white, except the mechanism inside the box frame.

2 Paint the box frame and the hearts panel F on Plan 2 apple green over the white primer.

3 Paint the mechanism with watered-down green paint

One dove is shown on a lower follower, with the heart between the side panel and hearts panel.

on the bare wood. A couple of coats should suffice. Sand down when dry.

4 Paint the front and edges of the three smaller hearts red.

5 Paint the two larger hearts, on the follower rods, red all over. Of course the rods themselves are green.

6 Paint the doves, referring to Plan 3, B. You will need brown, pink, grey, yellow and white paint, and a water-proof fine black pen for the beaks and eyes. Refer to the notes on transferring designs onto wood (*see* p.10).

Assembling the painted parts

1 All the drilled holes may need to be redrilled after painting, as they might have shrunk in the process.

2 Tap and glue the handle G on Plan 2 into the crank L. Glue the heart I to the crank as indicated.

3 Glue the collet K onto the shaft, up against the crank handle. This assembly may need repainting as one piece.

4 Insert the camshaft through the two bearings in the side panels. Temporarily fit the end-stop collet K onto the protruding end of the camshaft.

5 Wind the handle to ensure the shaft will turn freely in its bearings, then remove the end-stop collet and withdraw the camshaft.

6 Slide the four eccentric cam discs A on Plan 2, onto the camshaft. Position them roughly across the shaft, the two outer ones facing down and the two central cams facing up (or vice versa).

7 Insert the two follower rods, and their hearts, into the sides of the disc followers, Plan 3, A.

8 Fix the doves on the shaft G, with a friction fit, into the two disc followers. Don't glue them as you may wish to adjust them later.

9 Arrange the cams on the shaft to engage the outer edges of the followers. Once you have tested the mechanism, glue them as in the diagram on Plan 1.

10 Glue the end-stop collet J to the end of the projecting camshaft.

11 Glue the hearts panel F on Plan 2 in position as shown on Plan 1.

12 Operate the mechanism, clockwise or anti-clockwise, to check that when the hearts are apart so are the doves. When the hearts' follower rods face in, so do the doves.

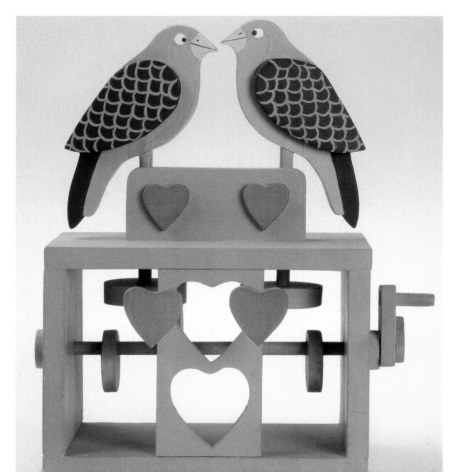

Both doves are shown on raised followers, with both hearts checked by the hearts panel, in the centre, from moving the doves out of position.

The hearts and doves are also controlled from moving out of position by the side panels.

Plan 3

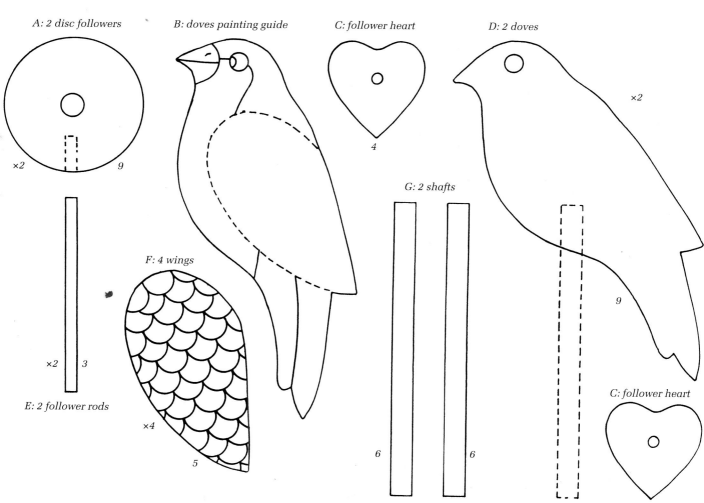

A: 2 disc followers

B: doves painting guide

C: follower heart

D: 2 doves

×2

×2   9

4

G: 2 shafts

F: 4 wings

E: 2 follower rods

×2   3

×4

5

6   6

9

C: follower heart

4

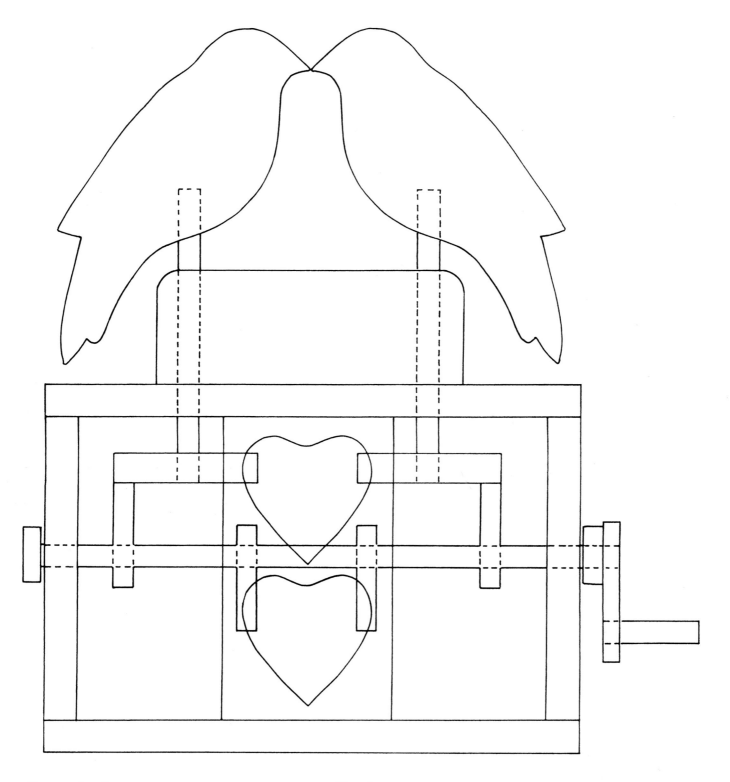

Construction diagram.   **Plan 1**

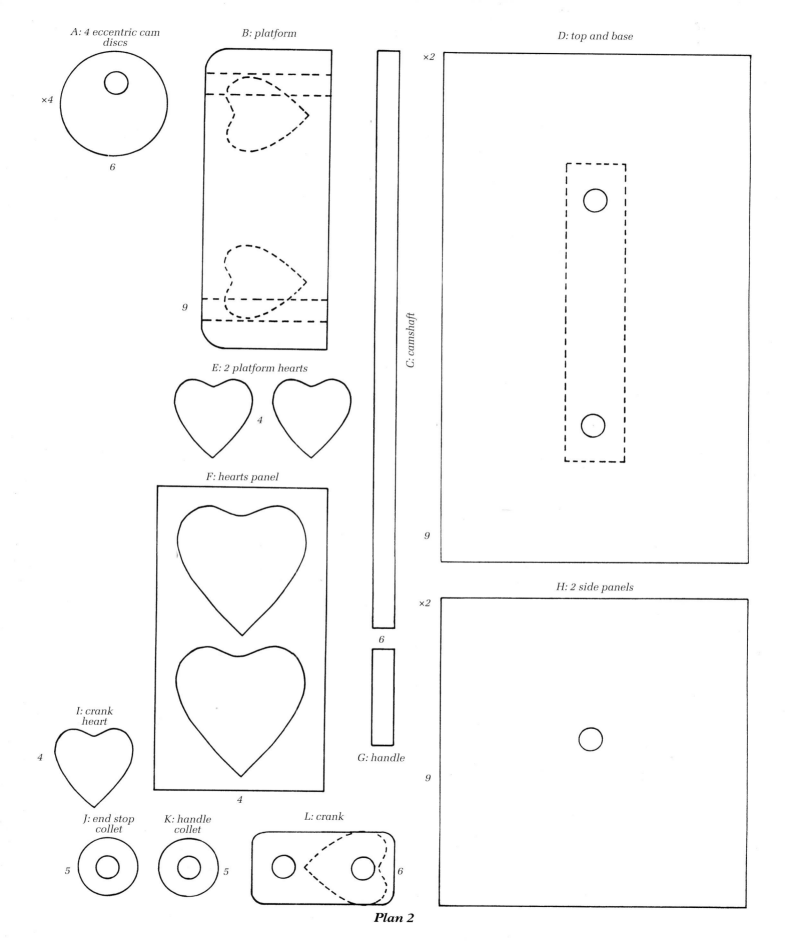

A: 4 eccentric cam discs

×4

6

B: platform

9

C: camshaft

6

D: top and base

×2

9

E: 2 platform hearts

4

F: hearts panel

4

G: handle

H: 2 side panels

×2

9

I: crank heart

4

J: end stop collet

5

K: handle collet

5

L: crank

6

Plan 2

8 ELEPHANT MESSENGER

The message, by airmail of course, is written on a Valentine card held in the elephant's trunk. He has wings for ears, unlike Disney's famous baby pachyderm 'Dumbo', who had ears for wings. His message is urgent – very urgent it would seem, from the messenger's frantic flapping and the way he leaps among the clouds. Wind the crank forward or backwards and the wings go up and down while the legs kick back and forth.

This is not one for beginners. There are five pages of plans and much to absorb. The painting should not be too daunting as sponging acrylic paint produces a good cloud effect and the hearts are stencilled. The mechanics, if not daunting, are quite testing, but well worth the effort.

MATERIALS

PLYWOOD	260 × 300 × 9mm (10.24 × 11.81 × 0.36in)	Box (crank and pivot block)
	220 × 300 × 9mm (8.66 × 11.81 × 0.36in)	Three elephant bodies, four elephant legs
AEROPLY		
	450 × 340 × 1.5mm (17.72 × 13.38 × 0.06in)	Cloud panels, wings
SOFTWOOD	50 × 120 × 20mm (1.97 × 4.72 × 0.79in)	Cloud counterweight
STRIPWOOD	19 × 180 × 9mm (0.75 × 7.09 × 0.36in)	Cranks, pivot block
DOWEL	40 × 20mm (1.58 × 0.79in)	Collets
	180 × 9mm (7.09 × 0.36in)	Crankshaft, crank pin
	330 × 5mm (13.11 × 0.20in)	Shaft, leg bars
PIANO WIRE	680 × 1mm (26.77 × 0.04in)	Leg rods, wing rods
BRASS TUBING	50 × 2mm (1.97 × 0.08in)	Wing supports

Four screw eyes
Airmail sticker
Cork tile 3mm (0.12in) thick

Elephant Messenger.
321 × 229 × 191mm (12.64 × 9.01 × 7.52in).

Making the box frame

1 Refer to the instructions regarding making boxes (*see* pp12–13).
2 Cut out two side panels A on Plan 1 from plywood. If possible, cut both simultaneously by temporarily bonding two pieces of plywood.

3 Drill a 10mm (0.4in) hole for the bearing through the two sides before separating them.
4 Cut out the base A on Plan 2 from plywood.
5 Cut out the platform B on Plan 3 from plywood.
6 Drill 1mm (0.04in) pilot holes for the screw eyes C and screw them into the platform as indicated by the dotted lines.
7 Drill a 9mm (0.36in) hole for the shaft.
8 Cut out the two baffle-blocks E from a 3mm (0.12in) cork tile to soften the sound.
9 Glue the baffle-blocks to the dotted line areas marked on the platform.
10 Make the box frame by gluing and pinning the sides to the base and platform.

Cutting out and fixing the cloud panels

1 Cut out the two side cloud panels E on Plan 5, from 1.5mm (0.06in) Aeroply. Cut both simultaneously by temporarily bonding them and leave them together.
2 Drill a 10mm (0.4in) hole for the bearing through them, which should exactly match those drilled in the side panels.
3 Separate the cloud panels and then glue and pin them to the sides of the box. Make sure you get them the right way round – the highest clouds nearest the front.
4 Now, cut out the front and rear cloud panels A on Plan 4 from Aeroply. Cut both simultaneously by temporarily bonding them together, then separate them.
5 Pin the panels to the front and back edges of the box frame. The larger clouds facing you are on the right, as on Plan 4. Don't glue them into position at this stage.
6 Cut out the cloud counterweight D on Plan 3 from softwood.
7 Drill a central 6mm (0.24in) hole in its side edge and two 1mm (0.04in) holes either side, as indicated on Plan 3.

Making the elephant's body

1 Cut out three elephant bodies B on Plan 1 from 9mm (0.36in) plywood, simultaneously if possible.
2 Drill two 7mm (0.28in) holes through the three elephant bodies, for the leg bars.
3 Drill two 1mm (0.04in) holes by the dotted line. If the drill bit is not long enough to go all the way

through all three elephants, drill again from the reverse side.
4 Separate the bodies. On the central body, cut away the rectangle bounded by the dotted line of the stomach as shown on B Plan 1.
5 Drill a 6mm (0.24in) hole on the central body at the angle and depth shown on Plan 1, B. Drill a 2mm (0.08in) hole for the tail.
6 Cut the slot for the Valentine card D in the end of the trunk.
7 Cut away the trunks on the two outer bodies, so that they match Plan 2, E. Sand these down so that they taper flush with the central trunk.
8 Glue and pin one truncated body to the central body (the elephant with the full trunk). The other truncated body should be temporarily bonded onto the body. Sand the edges of the cut trunks down smoothly so that when they are primed and painted the join will not be visible. (The illustrations show the join because the side is removed to expose the interior mechanism.)

Making the wings and legs

1 Cut out the wings G on Plan 3.
2 Drill 1mm (0.04in) holes in the wings.
3 Insert the screw eyes into the wings with thick super-glue. Snip off the protruding ends and file down smooth.

The truncated outer flank of the elephant will grow a full trunk once it is glued to its central section.

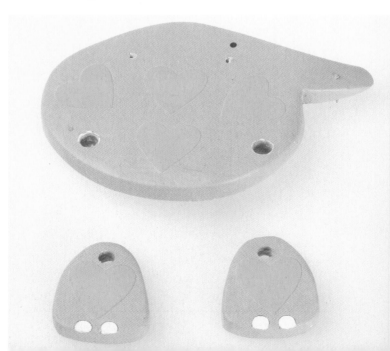

4 Saw off two 2mm (0.08in) pieces of brass tubing on Plan 3 for the wing support tubes H.

5 Ensure the ends are filed off smoothly. Superglue the brass tubes to the wings as indicated by the dotted line.

6 Cut two front legs, together, from B on Plan 2.

7 Cut two back legs together, from C on Plan 2. (The identical legs on Plan 4 are stencil cutting guides.)

8 Drill 6mm (0.24in) holes in the legs, just above the hearts, before separating them.

Making the handle and crankshaft

1 Cut the crank handle F, the first part of the crankshaft G and second part of the crankshaft H, all from dowel on Plan 4.

2 From stripwood, cut the three cranks I, J and K and pivot block D on Plan 4.

3 Drill 9mm (0.36in) holes in the cranks only, as indicated.

4 Drill a 10mm (0.4in) hole in the pivot block D and a 6mm (0.24in) hole in the top of the block to the depth indicated by the dotted line.

5 Tap and glue the handle F into the crank K.

6 Tap and glue the second part of the crankshaft H into the open hole in the crank K.

7 Slide the handle collet C on Plan 1 onto the second part of the crankshaft H and glue it to crank K.

The underside of a wing shows a screw eye waiting for a wing rod to be attached. A spindle in a brass tube support enables the wing to flap when inserted into a flank.

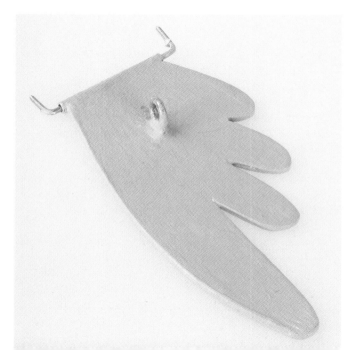

8 Tap (but don't glue) the end of the second part of the crankshaft H into the crank J on Plan 4 with a tight friction fit.

9 Tap the crank pin E into the hole in crank J.

10 Now, tap the crank pin E into the third crank I, leaving enough space between the cranks for the pivot block D to move freely on the pin.

11 Tap the first part of the crankshaft G into the open hole in crank I. The crankshaft is now assembled, except for the collet D on Plan 1 which will be added next to the bearing at the gluing stage.

Making the legs mechanism

1 Cut the two leg bars F on Plan 5 from dowel.

2 Drill central 1mm (0.04in) holes in their centres.

3 Screw two screw eyes C into the holes in the bars.

4 Remove the temporarily bonded flank of the elephant.

5 Insert the front leg bar, with its screw eye, through the front leg hole of the elephant. Temporarily fit a front leg flush with the protruding end of the bar.

6 Now do the same for the rear leg.

7 Insert the other ends of the two leg bars through the removable flank, which should now be temporarily bonded to the figure again.

8 Temporarily fit on the other front and rear legs to check that the bars' ends are flush with the leg surfaces. Once satisfied, remove the legs and the flank.

9 Work on leg bars in the cut away section can now begin.

10 Cut two 1mm (0.04in) lengths of piano wire for the leg rods B from Plan 5.

11 With small nosed pliers, twist loops into the ends of the wires to hook into the screw eyes on the leg rods. Pinch the loops shut.

12 Cut two end stops D. Drill 1mm (0.04in) holes in them. Fit the stops, but don't glue them to the wires.

Making the shaft mechanism

1 Cut the shaft A on Plan 5 from 6mm (0.24in) dowel.

2 Insert and glue the shaft into the hole you drilled, at an angle, into the central body on Plan 1.

3 Using a round file, enlarge the hole in the platform B on Plan 3, at an angle, into an oval shape.

4 Insert the shaft A on Plan 5 through the cloud counterweight D on Plan 3, the oval hole in the platform and into the pivot block D on Plan 4.

5 Ensure that the shaft moves freely back and forth within the enlarged platform bearing.

Making the wing mechanism

1 Cut the wing rods A on Plan 3 from 1mm (0.04in) piano wire.

2 Secure the wing rods to the screw eyes on the underside of the wings by twisting the end of the wire into loops.

3 Cut the wing spindles F on Plan 3 from 1mm (0.04in) piano wire.

4 Insert the spindles through the brass wing support tubes H attached to the end of the wings.

5 Bend the wires at right angles as marked by the two dots (leaving 10mm (0.4in) to insert into the holes).

6 Press the ends of the spindles into the small holes drilled for them, allowing plenty of space for the wings to move up and down freely.

7 Insert the ends of the wing rods into the cloud counterweight D on Plan 3, as indicated by the dotted line. Don't glue them at this stage, but you can test the mechanism.

Priming and painting

1 Follow the instructions for painting (*see* p.11).

2 Take apart all the assembled bits and pieces except for the leg bars and rods and the wing rods where they are fixed to the screw eyes. However, the wing rods should be removed from the cloud counterweight.

3 Temporarily pin the front and back cloud panels onto the box frame using the same pinholes as before.

4 Paint matt white (vinyl) emulsion to prime the wooden surfaces except for the crankshaft, shaft, leg bars and end stops which are inside the box.

5 Paint the cloud panels and cloud counterweight light blue.

6 Paint the elephant's body wings and legs, grey.

7 Cut a piece of 2mm (0.08in) string for the tail. Tie a knot in the string leaving a bit at the end to be spread out. Paint the tail grey, keeping it straight.

8 Paint the collet stop D on Plan 1 white (note that it is already primed white).

9 Paint the handle pink and its crank grey.

Stencilling and sponging

1 Cut out a photocopy of the elephant's legs stencil guides B and C on Plan 4. Spray-glue their backs and burnish down onto paper.

2 Cut out the reinforced stencil guide for the front legs B and back legs C.

3 With a stencil brush, dab on pink paint for the hearts and white paint for the toes. Apply the paint sparingly to avoid bleeding under the stencil, and use two coats.

4 Now comes the creative part. Cut a sponge 50mm (1.97in) square (or thereabouts) and dab it into (preferably acrylic) white paint. Make sure it is not too wet. Gently dab over the blue ground to get a good cloud effect. If necessary, you can retouch with blue using a brush. It is a good idea to experiment with sponging before you start on the actual piece.

5 Cut the Valentine card D on Plan 2 from postcard thickness white card. Stencil a pink heart and affix an air-mail sticker over it. Write your message on the inside of the card.

Assembling the crankshaft

1 Insert the second part of the crankshaft H on Plan 4, with its painted handle, through the right-hand side cloud panel.

2 Slide the collet stop D on Plan 1 onto the crankshaft. Don't glue it yet as adjustments will need to be made first.

3 Position the cranks I and J on Plan 4, with the pivot block D moving freely between them, on the crank pin E which is inserted flush with the cranks.

4 Pull out the crankshaft so that the first part of it G can be inserted into crank I and into the bearing of the left-hand inside panel.

5 The crankshaft can now operate, so glue the collet stop D on Plan 1 to the crankshaft, leaving 2mm (0.08in) play between it and the inside of the right-hand side panel.

6 Now, superglue all around the crankshaft where it meets the holes in the cranks.

OPPOSITE

ABOVE LEFT: A detail of the legs' mechanism shows the central section cut away to house the two leg bars with screw eyes attached to leg rods. The shaft supporting the elephant passes through the cloud counterweight to the mechanism below.

ABOVE RIGHT: A detail shows a leg rod inserted through a screw eye, with the end stop attached.

BELOW LEFT: A wing rod shows a loop ready to be secured to a screw eye on the underside of a wing. The two small holes for the spindle ends can be seen either side of the rod.

BELOW RIGHT: A side view shows a wing rod attached to a screw eye in the wing. When the wings are up, the legs are down.

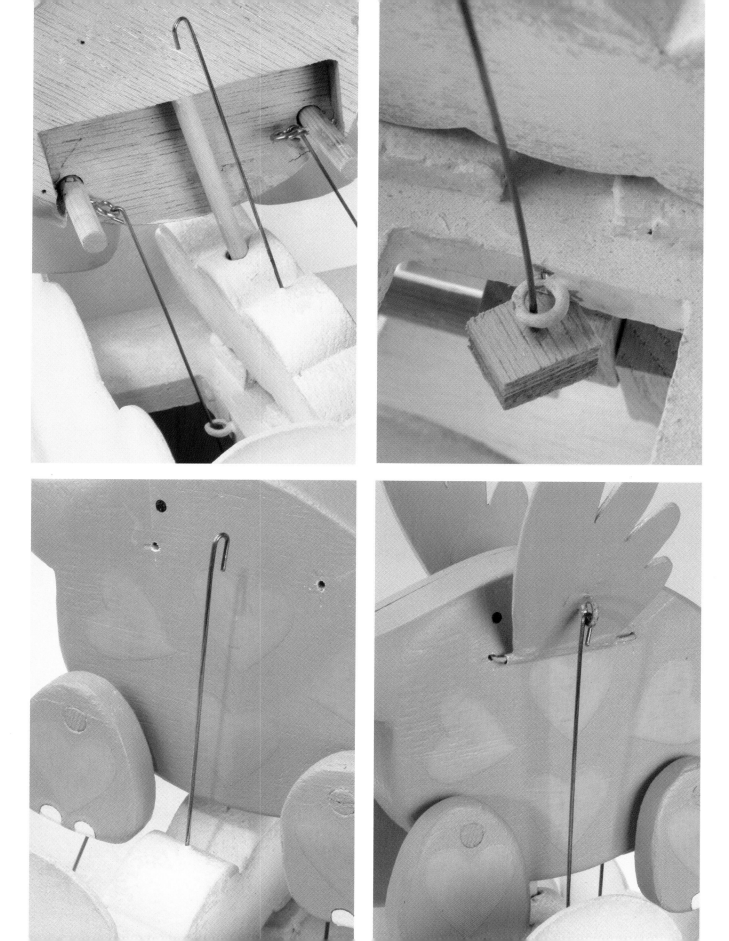

Assembling the shaft, rods and stops

1 Insert the shaft A on Plan 5 (imbedded in the elephant) through the central hole in the cloud counterweight D on Plan 3 and glue into the pivot block D on Plan 4. At the same time, feed the leg rods through the screw eyes fixed to the platform and superglue the wing rods into the cloud counterweight.

2 Insert the leg bars F, with their screw eyes, into the elephant's leg holes so that the ends project through the side. Friction-fit the legs onto the bars but don't glue them yet.

3 Superglue the end stops D on Plan 5 to the ends of the piano wire leg rods B so that they operate the legs back and forth. You will need to remove the back and front cloud panels to do this.

4 Adjust the leg movements so that the end stops pull up the legs when they reach the platform.

5 When satisfied with the forward and backward thrust of the legs, superglue the end stops to their wires.

6 Now glue all the legs into their positions on the leg bars as you tested them.

7 Glue and pin the removable flank to the centre section thereby sealing the leg mechanism.

8 Retouch with filler and paint to ensure that the joins at the base of the trunk are invisible.

9 Insert and superglue the wing spindles into their holes in the body, ensuring that the wings move freely.

10 At the back of the elephant, glue in the stiff straight grey tail. Slot the Valentine's card into the end of the trunk and glue it into position.

11 Glue and pin (in the existing holes) the front and rear cloud panels to the edges of the box frame. Wind the crank and the 'Elephant Messenger' will, with much effort, deliver your message.

The cloud effect is achieved by dry sponging white paint over light blue. The hearts and toes are stencilled on with the aid of cutting guides.

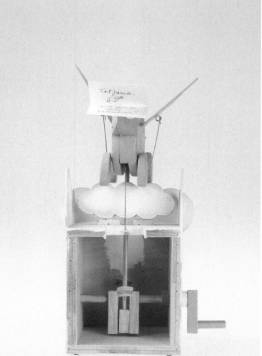

The crankshaft houses a pivot block for the shaft which turns on a crank pin between the two cranks. When the wings are up the elephant is down.

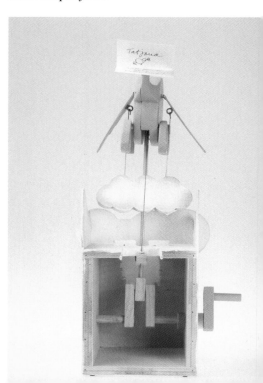

And when the wings are down the elephant is up. The crank slider mechanism, which operates in a bearing in the platform, thrusts the elephant back and forth using the cloud counterweight to operate the wings. The end stops on the leg rods pull up the legs when the stops reach the platform.

A: 2 side panels

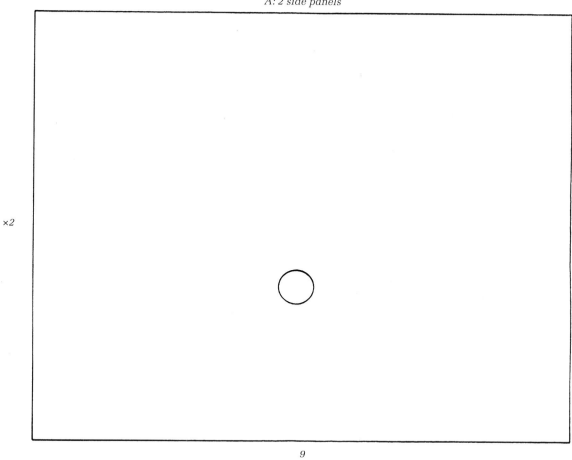

×2

9

B: body's central section

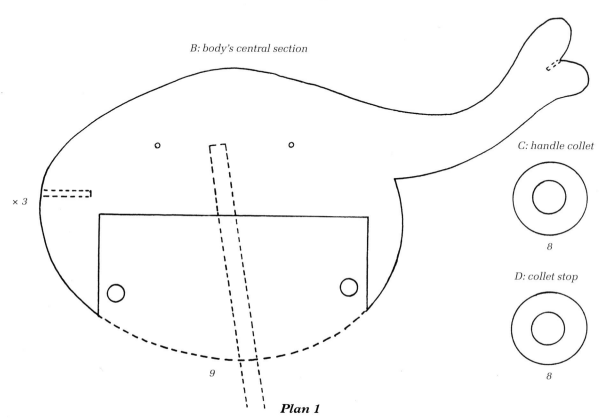

× 3

9

C: handle collet

8

D: collet stop

8

Plan 1

A: base

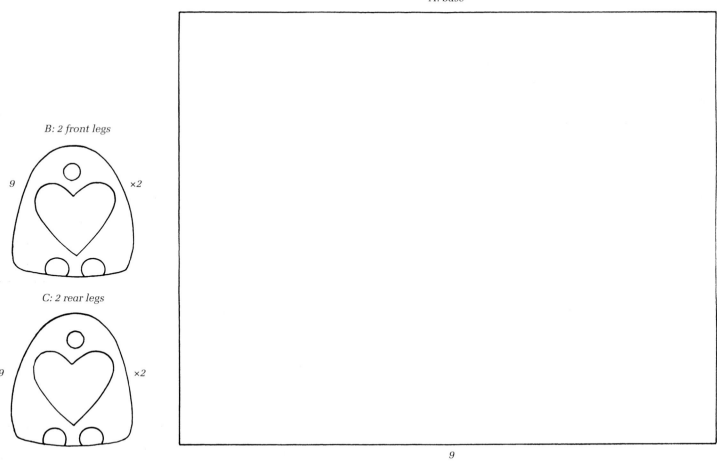

9

B: 2 front legs

9   ×2

C: 2 rear legs

9   ×2

D: Valentine card

BY AIR MAIL
par avion
Royal Mail

E: body stencil guide

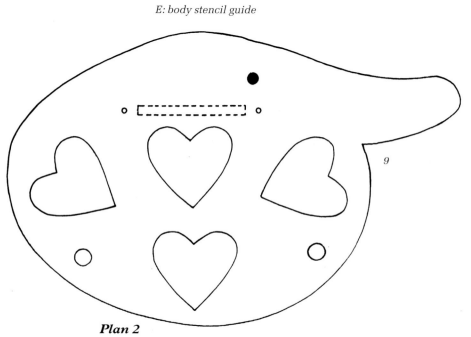

9

Plan 2

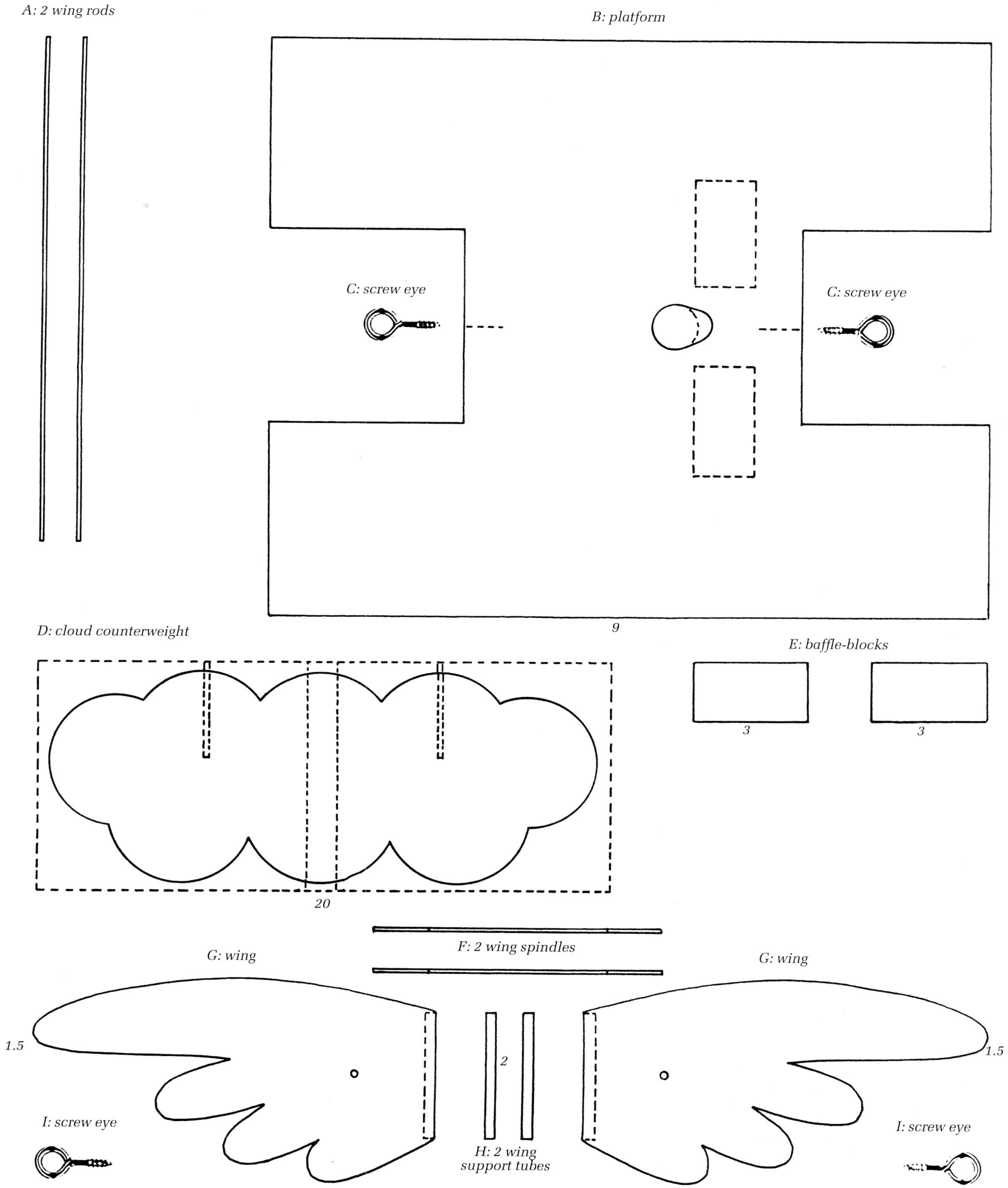

A: 2 wing rods

B: platform

C: screw eye

C: screw eye

D: cloud counterweight

E: baffle-blocks

3

3

9

20

F: 2 wing spindles

G: wing

G: wing

1.5

1.5

I: screw eye

H: 2 wing
support tubes

2

I: screw eye

Plan 3

A: 2 front and rear cloud panels

×2

B: front leg stencil
guide

C: rear leg
stencil guide

E: crank pin

D: pivot block

9

9

1.5

F: crank handle

G: lst part of crankshaft

H: 2nd part of crankshaft

9

9

9

I: crank

J: crank

K: crank

9

9

9

Plan 4

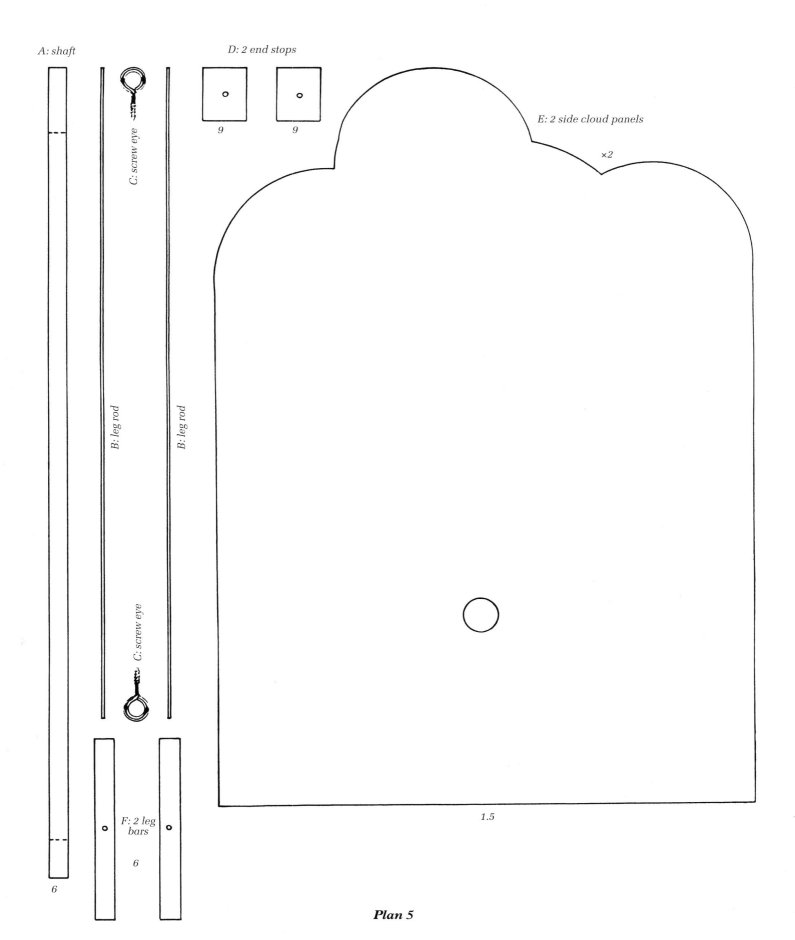

A: shaft

D: 2 end stops

E: 2 side cloud panels

C: screw eye

B: leg rod

B: leg rod

C: screw eye

F: 2 leg bars

9

9

×2

1.5

6

6

6

Plan 5

9 ARK TOY

This is a toddler's toy with a magic mechanism: the Geneva wheel. It works on the same principle as a film projector, stepping the film on one frame at a time. As the crank is turned (clockwise or anti-clockwise), at each revolution different animals appear on deck, with a pause between each.

It is a simple matching game using both shapes and colour. Each animal is duplicated exactly, except for the lions. It is a fairly easy toy to make but a ruling pen and a pair of compasses will be required to paint the rainbow.

MATERIALS

PLYWOOD	270 × 192 × 9mm (10.63 × 7.56 × 0.36in)	Base, rainbow
	435 × 186 × 6mm (17.13 × 7.32 × 0.24in)	Waves, animals, hull panels
AEROPLY	250 × 90 × 1.5mm (9.84 × 3.54 × 0.06in)	Deck, sides
DOWEL	30 × 15mm (1.18 × 0.59in)	Collet
	100 × 4mm (3.94 × 0.16in)	Spindle, handle, crankshaft
	410 × 3mm (16.15 × 0.12in)	Spacers, crank pin
STRIPWOOD	140 × 42 × 5mm (5.5 × 1.66 × 0.20in)	Crank wheel, shield, cross, wheel, crank

Cutting out the rainbow, waves and base

1 Spray-glue the photocopies of the plans onto plywood as indicated.
2 Cut the rainbow B on Plan 1 from plywood. Do not, however, at this stage cut out the interior inverted 'U' shape. You will need this to support your compasses in the central dot. Prick this now for future use and remove the photocopy, but keep it for reference of the spacing for the concentric bands.
3 Cut out the front and rear waves D on Plan 1, together if possible, from plywood.
4 Cut out two port waves A on Plan 1, together, from plywood.
5 Cut out two more port waves, separately or together, from I and O on Plan 2 from 6mm (0.24in) plywood.

Ark Toy.
191 × 171 × 76mm (7.52 × 6.74 × 2.99in).

6 Cut out two starboard waves C on Plan 1, together, from plywood.
7 Cut out two more starboard waves H and Q on Plan 2, separately or together, from plywood.
8 Cut out the base G on Plan 3 from plywood.

Cutting out the hull panels and deck

1 Cut out the front and rear hull panels L on Plan 2 from plywood. If possible cut them simultaneously by temporarily bonding the pieces together.
2 Drill ten 3mm (0.12in) holes through the two panels, as indicated, around the perimeter. It is important that they are straight and so they are best drilled with a pillar drill or at least a drill stand attachment for your drill.
3 Drill two 5mm (0.20in) holes in the centre of the hull panels, as indicated.
4 Cut ten spacer bars F on Plan 2 from dowel.
5 Take the two hull panels apart. Tap and glue the bars

into their holes on the inside of the front panel. The hull is not quite symmetrical so it is important the bars are fixed to the inside, not the outside of the panel.

6 Now, tap the rear panel (facing the same way as the front panel) onto the spacer bars, but don't glue them in yet. A temporary friction-fit is sufficient.

7 Cut the two side panels F on Plan 3 from Aeroply.

8 Glue these side panels to the edges of the front hull panel, but not to the temporarily fixed rear hull panel. (You will need to work inside the hull later.)

9 Cut out the deck J on Plan 2 from Aeroply.

10 Cut out the interior slot in the deck with a craft knife.

11 Glue the fore edge of the underside of the deck to the top edge of the front hull panel and the side edge to the tops of the side panels. (This hasn't been done on the illustrations as the components have to be dismantled.)

Cutting out the animals

1 On Plan 3 cut out from plywood, the deck animals: bear A; elephant B; tiger C; lioness D; and hippo E. Drill 2mm (0.08in) holes for the string tails as indicated.

2 Cut out the animals' rotary disc E on Plan 2 from one piece of plywood.

3 Cut the animals free from the rotary disc along their feet. Keep the off-cut as this will be your template for gluing the animals back into their original positions once you have drilled tail holes and cut between their legs.

4 Cut out the spaces between the legs (except for the bear which doesn't have any space to cut).

5 Drill 2mm (0.08in) tail holes in the hippo, elephant and lion as indicated.

6 Glue 1.5mm (0.06in) thick string tails into the holes. Tie knots in their tails, referring to the illustrations.

7 Drill a central 4mm (0.16in) hole in the 'U' shaped disc.

8 Using the off-cut from the animals' rotary disc as a guide, glue the animals' feet back into their original positions on the disc. Ensure that the figures lie flat against the surface.

Making the Geneva wheel mechanism

1 Cut out the cross A, the shield B and the crank wheel G on Plan 2 from stripwood.

2 Drill central 4mm (0.16in) holes in the cross, shield and crank wheel and a 3mm (0.12in) hole near the edge of the crank wheel, as shown.

3 Cut out the crankshaft C on Plan 2 from dowel.

4 Cut the crank pin D from dowel. Glue and insert it into the small hole on the outer edge of the crank wheel G.

The animals' rotary disc shows the animals, with tails attached, cut from one piece of plywood. The cross on the disc completes the Geneva wheel mechanism.

5 Insert and glue the crankshaft C into the shield B flush with the end.

6 Insert the crankshaft through the crank wheel G and glue the shield, on the end of it, as shown by the dotted line.

7 Glue the collet N onto the spindle K 7mm (0.28in) from its end (not including the width of the collet).

8 Glue the cross A on Plan 2 onto the animals' rotary disc E in the position indicated by the dotted line.

9 Cut out the crank P from stripwood. Drill two 4mm (0.16in) holes as indicated.

10 Cut the handle M from dowel. Tap and glue it into the hole in the crank.

Testing the Geneva wheel mechanism

1 Insert the crankshaft, with its crank wheel, shield and crank pin glued to it, through the lower hole on the inside of the front hull panel. Temporarily secure it by friction-fitting the handle onto the end.

2 Insert the spindle, with the cross glued to the animals' rotary disc, into the upper hole on the inside of the front hull panel.

3 Turn the crank handle so that the shield engages the cross by fitting into a concave recess.

4 Friction-fit the rear hull panel, temporarily, onto the spacer bars glued to the front hull panel, ensuring it faces the same way as the front panel. (The lower hole serves no purpose, since it was merely drilled together with the front hull panel and will be hidden.)

The rainbow stands on a base, glued and supported by the rear wave. The sea effect is achieved by using a wet sponge dipped in blue paint over a white primer.

Priming and painting

1 Prime the rainbow B on Plan 1 with matt white (vinyl) emulsion, but don't paint over the central pricked hole for your compass. Refer to the general notes on painting and sponging (*see* pp11–12).

2 Prime the front and side edges of the base, the hull and the side panels white. Do likewise with the waves, crank and crank handle. Leave the deck and animals unprimed.

3 Use a ruling pen and compass to draw the concentric bands of colour in the rainbow: red, orange, yellow, green, blue and violet. Fill in with a brush, using at least two coats.

4 When dry, cut out the inverted 'U' shape and sand down. Prime the inside edge of the bare wood white, and paint a couple of coats of violet over it.

5 Stain the animals, directly onto plywood, with muted liquid colours. This acts as a foil to the brightly coloured rainbow. Bears are light brown; elephants are light grey; tigers are light yellow and lions are indian yellow with a light brown mane for the male. The hippo is light blue (my hippos always are!).

6 Stain the tail the same colour as the animals. Arrange the tails as in the illustration and glue them in place.

7 Cut a sponge 50mm (1.97in) square, and wet it.

8 Dab wet blue paint on the white primed waves to achieve a mottled watery effect, with plenty of white showing through.

9 Paint the hull and crank handle indian yellow, much the same colour as the unpainted and unprimed deck.

Assembling the rainbow and waves

1 Glue the rainbow, along the dotted line, to the rear of the base G on Plan 3.

2 Support the rainbow by gluing the rear wave against it, along the second dotted line.

3 Glue the front wave (the nicer of the two) onto the base, flush with the front side and edges, along the third dotted line.

4 Glue four, evenly spaced, port waves on the left, flush with the edge of the base.

5 Glue four, evenly spaced, starboard waves on the right, flush with the edge of the base.

Overhead detail of the waves shows the even spacing between them. Port waves on the left are shaped differently to starboard waves on the right.

Assembling the 'Ark Toy'

1 This stage is mainly a re-run of testing the mechanism, with the components glued into position.

2 Insert the crankshaft (with its components attached) through the lower hole on the inside of the front hull panel.

3 Glue the crank handle to the protruding end of the crankshaft ensuring that it still moves freely in its bearing now that it has been painted.

4 Insert the spindle attached to the animals' rotary disc into the upper hole on the inside of the front hull panel. Ensure that the round part of the shield engages the concave part of the cross and that it moves freely in its bearing.

5 Test the mechanism. (This will be the last chance to make alterations.)

6 Dab glue onto the ten inside holes in the rear hull panel, around the perimeter.

7 Glue the outside edges of the rear hull panel, except its bottom edge.

8 Fit the rear hull panel, matching the front panel, onto the ten spacer bars ensuring that it lines up squarely with the side panels and deck.

9 Use masking tape to ensure that all the pieces glue and dry correctly. (Don't use the tape too soon after painting or it will peel off the paint!)

10 Glue the deck animals A–E on Plan 3 to the deck in their allotted positions, as shown on J, Plan 2.

11 Glue the insides of the front and rear waves within the boundaries of the hull, making sure that no glue goes beyond that point. Place the ark squarely in the well.

12 Turn the handle to the right and the animals go to the left, following each other in rotation. Thus a matching game for a toddler ensues.

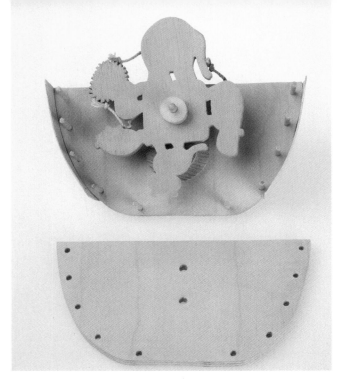

The side panels are glued to the edges of the front hull panel. The spacer bars are tapped and glued into it. The main part of the Geneva wheel mechanism shows the wheel and crank pin, on its outer edge.

BELOW LEFT: The reverse of the animals' rotary disc is secured by a collet on the spindle which fits into the upper hole in the inside of the rear hull panel, shown below.

BELOW: The deck animals are glued onto the deck last. The string tails are the same colours as the animals.

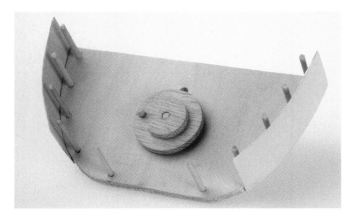

ABOVE: The completed hull with the crank handle shows five stationary animals and the lion and second bear in the centre, on the animals' rotary disc within the hull.

RIGHT: The completed 'Ark Toy' now shows a tiger on the rotary disc.

Plan 3

A: bear

B: elephant

C: tiger

F: 2 side panels

6

6

6

1.5

D: lioness

E: hippo

6

6

×2

G: base

9

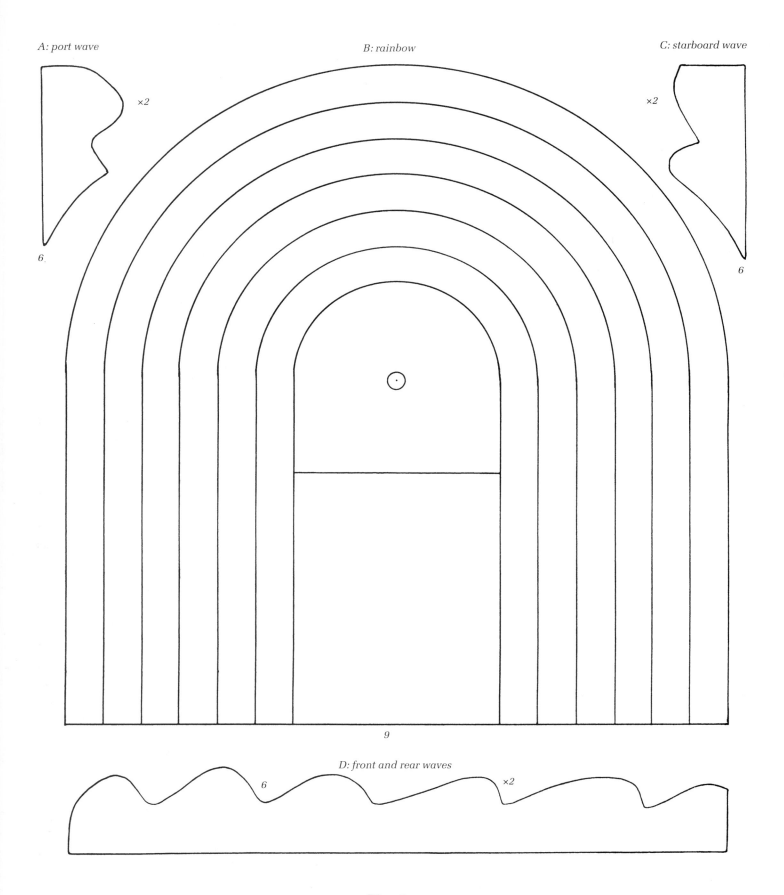

A: port wave

×2

6

B: rainbow

C: starboard wave

×2

6

9

D: front and rear waves

6

×2

Plan 1

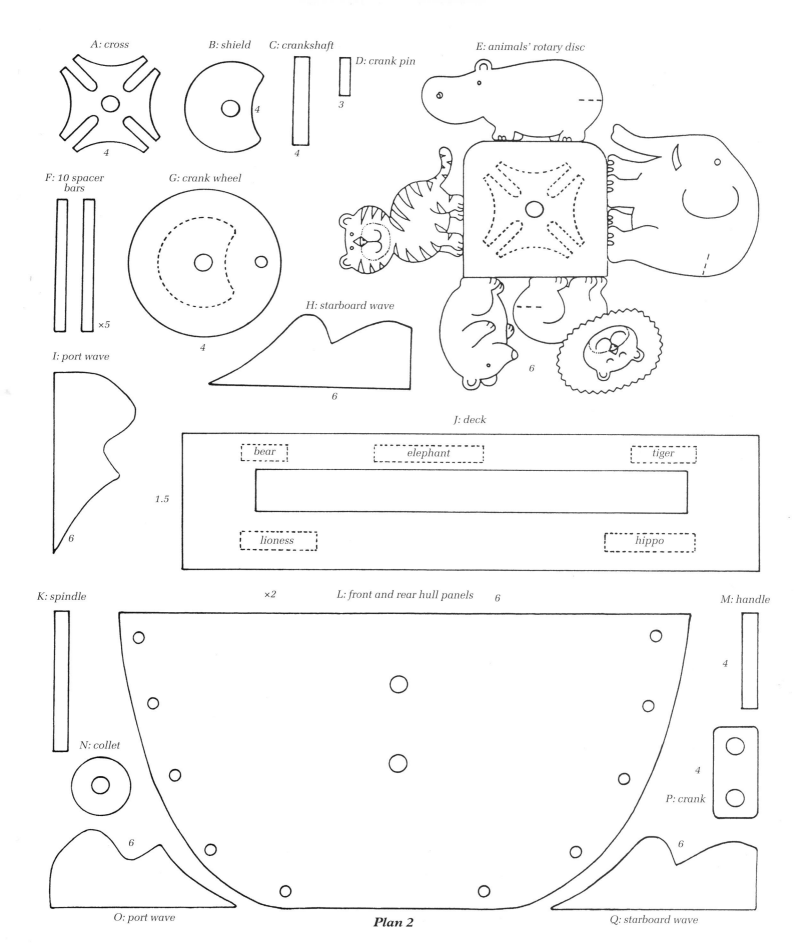

A: cross

4

B: shield

4

C: crankshaft

4

D: crank pin

3

E: animals' rotary disc

6

F: 10 spacer bars

×5

G: crank wheel

4

H: starboard wave

6

I: port wave

6

J: deck

bear   elephant   tiger

1.5

lioness   hippo

K: spindle

×2   L: front and rear hull panels   6

M: handle

4

N: collet

4

P: crank

6   6

O: port wave

Q: starboard wave

Plan 2

10 DANCING CHARLIE

Sir Charles Spencer Chaplin (1889–1977) was an English actor of comic genius. Stan Laurel described him as 'the greatest artist that was ever on the screen'. And yet it is not Charlie Chaplin who is the inspiration for this piece, but a mechanical toy musical box.

In the 1960s, London department stores sold dancing clowns with musical movements which, when wound up, performed remarkably convincing displays of dancing. They have since become collectors' items and, mechanically, throw the hook for this toy.

Artistically, Chaplin's wistful little tramp would seem to be the perfect choice to inhabit this small stage. He tap dances, stamps and sways from side to side, evoking the early silent era of the cinema. The secret of the dancing mechanism lies in an eccentric cam raising and lowering a perfectly balanced puppet with very long feet. The toes and heels control Charlie's random routine.

Photocopies of the plans provide the actual decoration which can be spray-glued onto plywood.

MATERIALS

PLYWOOD	405 × 255 × 9mm (15.95 × 10.04 × 0.36in)	Side panels, stage
	405 × 150 × 5mm (15.95 × 5.9 × 0.20in)	Proscenium, back and side panels
AEROPLY	420 × 195 × 1.5mm (16.54 × 7.67 × 0.06in)	Top and support guard, Charlie puppet, picture panel
SOFTWOOD	120 × 33 × 15mm (4.73 × 1.3 × 0.59)	Follower block
STRIPWOOD	50 × 10 × 6mm (1.97 × 0.4 × 0.24in)	Crank
DOWEL	40 × 28mm (1.58 × 1.10in)	Eccentric cam
	40 × 12mm (1.58 × 0.47in)	Collets
	210 × 6mm (8.27 × 0.24in)	Handle, camshaft

Four pop rivets
Extra photocopies as required

Cutting out the box

1 Cut out the proscenium A on Plan 1 from 5mm (0.20in) plywood, ignoring the tabs. (Just cut out the proscenium itself.)

Dancing Charlie.
184 × 191 × 113mm (7.25 × 7.52 × 4.45in).

2 Cut out the two side panels D on Plan 2 from plywood. Cut them simultaneously if possible by temporarily bonding the sheets together. Ignore the tabs.

3 Drill a 7mm (0.28in) bearing through both side panels. If they are temporarily bonded, they should now be separated.

4 Cut out the back panel C on Plan 3 from plywood. Dotted lines show the position for shelf A on Plan 4.

5 Cut out the top B on Plan 4 from Aeroply.

6 Cut out the stage B on Plan 3 from plywood.

7 Cut out the Charlie picture panel A on Plan 5 from Aeroply, leaving an extra 5mm (0.20in) all round.

Cutting out the photocopies

1 You will need photocopies of the proscenium A on Plan 1; two photocopies of the side panels D together with Charlie and his bits on Plan 2; one photocopy of the top B on Plan 4 and a photocopy of Charlie's picture panel on Plan 5.

2 Cut out the photocopy of the proscenium A on Plan 1 along the tabs.

3 Cut out two photocopies of the side panels D on Plan 2 along their tabs.

4 Cut out a photocopy of the top B on Plan 4 along its tabs.

The picture panel blow-up of Charlie Chaplin is glued to the shelf behind. It has a little slot to allow the holding pin to be inserted into the follower block and operate the puppet.

5 Cut out a photocopy of the picture panel A on Plan 5, but leave a 5mm (0.20in) white border all round.

6 Cut out a photocopy of Charlie and his bits on Plan 2.

Scoring and spray-gluing the photocopies

1 Place the photocopies, in turn, on a piece of cardboard and score along all the tabs for folding over.

2 Spray-glue the reverse sides of the prints. Do likewise to their corresponding ply components. Don't use a liquid glue, such as wallpaper paste, which allows the paper to stretch and loses accuracy.

3 Working on one panel at a time, position each panel over the appropriate print (on a light box if possible to achieve maximum accuracy) and carefully bring the glued surfaces together. Ensure the fit is exact before folding over the tabs onto the plywood panels. Burnish everything down firmly.

The side panel decorations show Charlie in various dancing positions.

4   The picture panel on Plan 5 has no tabs so the photo-copy must be cut leaving a 5mm (0.20in) white border all round.

5   Cut out a piece of Aeroply 182 × 140 × 1.5mm (7.17 × 5.5 × 0.06in) to match the size of the cut photocopy.

6   Spray-glue the reverse of the photocopy and of the Aeroply. When tacky, bond them together and burnish down firmly.

7   Using a craft knife, cut out the picture panel along its printed edge. Cut out the interior slot too.

8   Spray-glue the reverse of the photocopy showing Charlie's components on plan 2 and do likewise to a piece of Aeroply large enough to accommodate them.

9   When tacky, bring the surfaces together and burnish down firmly. Put this aside for now.

Gluing and pinning the box

1   Glue and pin the back panel C Plan 3 between the side panels D on Plan 2 so that the dotted rule is 81mm (3.19in) from the top, to be sure to get it the right way up.

2   Pierce the bearings in the papered side panels with a thick paintbrush with a tapering handle. Check that a piece of 6mm (0.24in) dowel can move easily within the bearings.

3   Before fixing the stage B on Plan 3, paint the top white and the front edge black.

4   When dry, glue and pin the stage to the back and side panels.

5   Glue and pin the proscenium to the edges of the other panels. Retouch the panel pinheads with black and white paint so that they don't show.

Making the shelf and support blocks

1   Cut the support blocks D on Plan 4 from softwood.

2   Cut out the shelf A on Plan 4 from plywood.

3   Cut out the interior slot on the continuous line in the middle. The dotted lines represent positioning for the support blocks either side and the support guard at the front.

4   Glue the two support blocks D on Plan 4 either side of the slot as indicated by the dotted line.

5   Cut out the support guard E from Aeroply and glue it to the ends of the support blocks as indicated.

6   Glue the shelf, on the back and side edges, squarely between the two dotted lines onto the back panel as shown on Plan 3.

Making the mechanism

1   Cut the follower block C on Plan 4 from softwood.

2   Drill a 2mm (0.08in) central hole in its front edge as indicated by the dotted line.

3   Cut the handle B on Plan 1 from dowel.

4   Cut out the crank C from stripwood. Drill two 6mm (0.24in) holes in it.

5   Cut two collets D from dowel. Drill 6mm (0.24in) holes in them.

6   Cut the eccentric cam E from dowel.

7   Cut the camshaft F from dowel.

Cutting out and assembling Charlie

1   Charlie has been waiting in the wings, glued to Aeroply. He can now be cut out, but great care needs to be taken over the delicate areas such as the cane, curls and bouquet, and in those areas leave a little white space. Paint the flowers with a translucent red ink or liquid paint so the black drawing shows through.

2   Use your saw blade as a file, nudging up to the delicate areas cutting away the waste.

3   Drill 2mm (0.08in) holes in the upper and lower legs and the body as indicated on Plan 2.

The stage is shaped to fit into the proscenium, back and side panels, when glued together.

4 Four pop rivets A Plan 3 need to be converted to make fixings for the limbs. First, with the aid of pliers and a small hammer, tap the sliding parts of the rivets until they come loose. Second, remove them from the rivet pins, but keep them handy.

5 Insert the four 'naked' pins through the chest; through the lower body into the upper legs; and through the upper legs into the lower legs.

6 Slide the detached parts back onto the rivet pins, but inverted now.

7 With the inverted heads pushed up against the limbs, ensure that the limbs themselves can move freely before snipping off three ends in the lower body and legs.

8 The fourth pin (in the chest) remains uncut, for this is the support pin for the body. Ensure that there is plenty of play so that the figure can move freely on the pin.

Charlie is perfectly balanced to perform evenly on either side.

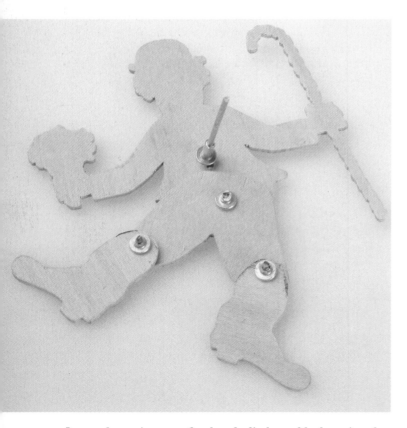

Inverted pop rivets are fixed to the limbs and body, snipped and superglued. The top inverted rivet remains uncut as it is the holding pin which is inserted into the follower block.

9 Dab superglue, vertically, onto the snipped off joints so that it penetrates the joints without leaking and sticking the limbs together! Ensure that the limbs move freely on the pins.

Assembling the mechanism

1 Tap and glue the handle B on Plan 1 into one of the holes in the crank C.

2 Tap and glue the camshaft F through collet D and into the other hole in the crank.

3 Paint the collet and crank white and the handle black.

4 Insert the camshaft into the bearing in the right-hand side panel, ensuring that it can turn freely in the bearing.

5 Slide the other collet D and the eccentric cam E onto the centre of the shaft while you fit the end into the bearing in the left-hand side panel.

6　Slide the collet to the right, 2mm (0.08in) from the side panel and glue it in position.

7　Drop the follower block C on Plan 4 (with its drilled hole at the bottom) into the shelf slot with the support blocks and guard.

8　Put some PVA glue (not superglue) into the hole at the bottom of the follower block ready to receive the support pin in Charlie's chest. Don't insert the pin at this point.

9　Glue the front edge of the shelf and slide in the picture panel from the top onto the stage. Ensure that it is at right angles to the proscenium.

10　Locate the hole in the follower block (which now contains PVA glue) through the little slot in the picture panel. Press in the support pin holding Charlie into the hole as far as the inverted rivet on the pin allows (about 10mm (0.40in) between Charlie and the picture panel).

11　Charlie should be perfectly balanced, with toes about 5mm (0.20in) off the ground at his highest point. Experiment by winding the crank and pulling the support pin further in or out to achieve the perfect dancing movements.

12　Finally, glue and pin the top B on Plan 4 to the tops of all four panels and Charlie is ready to perform.

OVERLEAF: A bird's eye view shows the follower block inserted in a slot in the shelf, sandwiched between two blocks and a support guard.

The mechanism shows the follower block, with a hole for the holding pin, resting on an eccentric cam. The cam, when turned, produces an up and down movement which, allied to the feet touching the stage, gives an unpredictable series of dance steps.

The highest position of the eccentric cam lifts the follower block 12mm (0.47in). The proscenium, sides and top are covered with photocopies of the graphics on the plans. Only the stage, flowers and crank handle are painted.

A: proscenium

CHARLIE

5

B: handle

6

C: crank

6

D: collets

4   4

E: eccentric cam

8

F: camshaft   6

Plan 1

A: upper legs

1.5

B: lower legs

1.5

C: body

1.5

D: side panels

×2

9

Plan 2

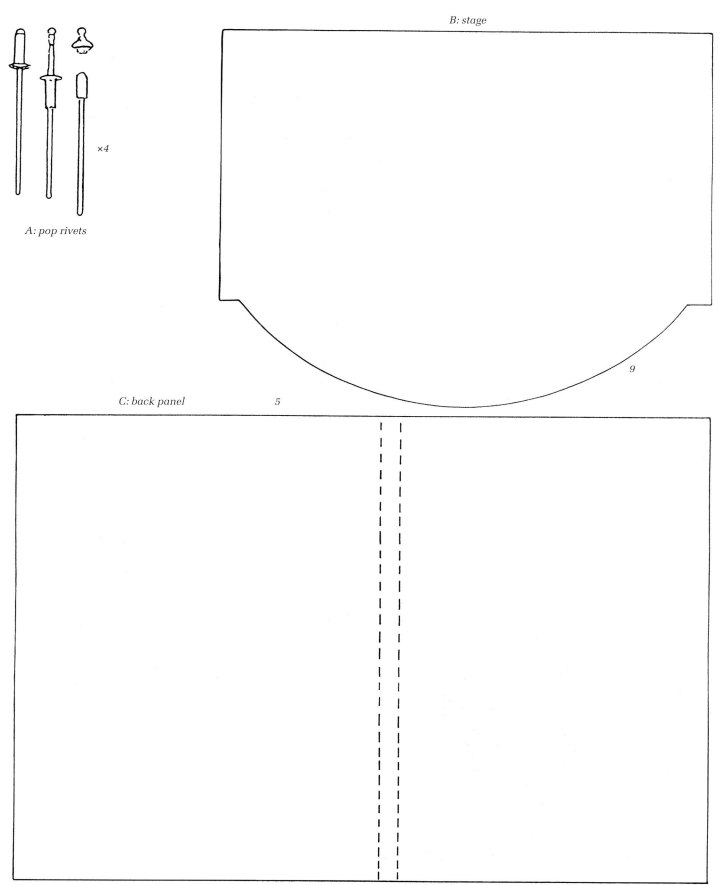

A: pop rivets

×4

B: stage

9

C: back panel

5

Plan 3

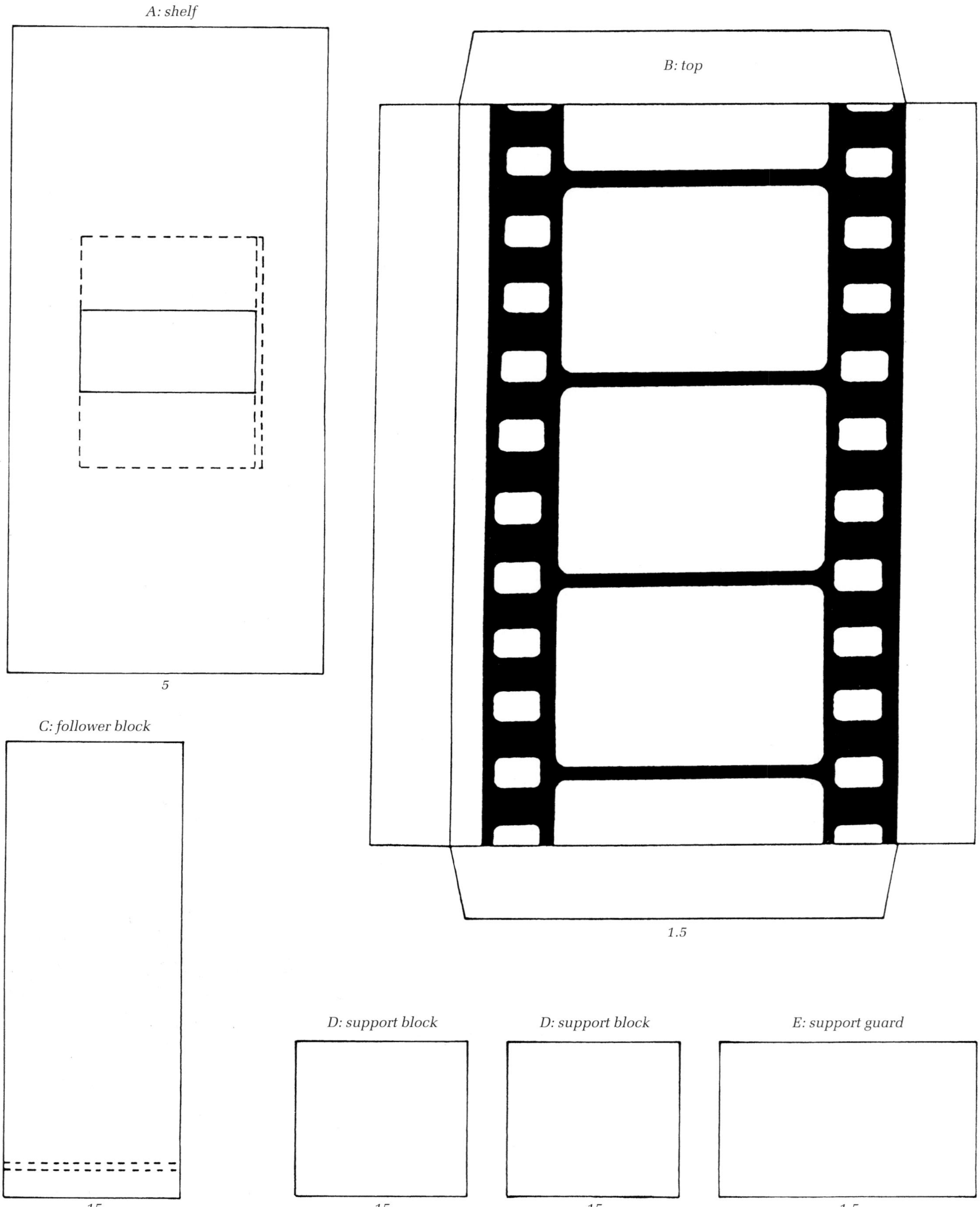

A: shelf

5

C: follower block

15

B: top

1.5

D: support block

15

D: support block

15

E: support guard

1.5

Plan 4

Picture panel

1.5

Plan 5

11 HOORAY FOR HOLLYWOOD!

The Hollywood sign is arguably the world's most famous graphic icon. When it was originally erected in 1924, rather than being a logo for the Californian film industry it was instead a real estate advertising sign reading 'HOLLY-WOODLAND'. The letters were 50 feet high, 30 feet wide and made of sheet metal, telephone poles, pipe wire and hundreds of 40 watt bulbs. Maintenance was a problem and it was allowed to deteriorate.

In 1949 the sign was restored to read: HOLLYWOOD and again it deteriorated, but was restored once more in 1978 at a cost of $27,000 per letter. Because of their position on the hillside the letters always appear to be moving. This toy, while reflecting that illusion, pays homage to the great, and even not so great, films to come out of the Dream Factory.

Mechanically, it is a simple toy to make with the letters riding up and down on a camshaft while the star spins round on a friction disc. It makes an intriguing shelf-piece, especially to those drawn to Hollywood, either as fans or participants.

MATERIALS

Material	Dimensions	Use
PLYWOOD	435 × 200 × 9mm (17.13 × 7.90 × 0.36in)	Platform and base, two side panels, star
	260 × 275 × 5mm (10.23 × 10.82 × 0.20in)	First and second parts of back panel
	210 × 40 × 4mm (8.27 × 1.58 × 0.16in)	Letters
AEROPLY	270 × 150 × 1.5mm (10.63 × 5.9 × 0.06in)	Front panel
BATTENING (PSE)	80 × 40 × 18mm (3.15 × 1.58 × 0.71in)	Friction block
	50 × 32 × 12mm (1.97 × 1.26 × 0.47in)	Two fascias
	250 × 22 × 12mm (9.84 × 0.87 × 0.47in)	Nine blocks
	240 × 12 × 12mm (9.45 × 0.47 × 0.47in)	Extra bearings bar
DOWEL	100 × 38mm (3.94 × 1.5in)	Nine eccentric cams, friction disc
	60 × 20mm (2.36 × 0.79in)	Collets
	330 × 8mm (12.99 × 0.32in)	Camshaft, handle
	250 × 6mm (9.84 × 0.24in)	Nine follower rods, friction rod
STRIPWOOD	50 × 20 × 6mm (1.97 × 0.79 × 0.24in)	Crank

Stencil brush
Extra photocopies of Plans 1 and 4

Hooray for Hollywood!
229 × 341 × 87mm (9.01 × 13.43 × 3.43in).

Cutting the box and back panel

1 Cut the front panel D on Plan 1 from Aeroply.
2 Cut out two side panels A on Plan 2 from plywood. Cut both simultaneously, if possible, by temporarily bonding two pieces of plywood.

3   Drill a 9mm (0.36in) bearing through both panels. If they were temporarily bonded, separate them now.

4   Cut out, together if possible, the platform and base A on Plan 3 from plywood.

5   Cut out photocopies of the first part of the back panel B on Plan 3 and the second part of the back panel C on Plan 4. Join them together at the dotted lines and spray the backs. Stick the joined sheets onto plywood and cut out the back panel in one piece.

Making the crank handle and camshaft

1   Cut out the crank C on Plan 2 from stripwood. Drill two 8mm (0.32in) holes in it.

2   Cut out the handle D from dowel. Tap and glue it

The back panel is removed to show the assembly of eccentric cams' profiles supporting the follower rods attached to the letter blocks.

Detail of the friction-driven rod which turns the star when inserted into the friction block.

Detail of the crank handle and collet showing also the eccentric cams arranged to give a lively performance of the letters moving up and down.

into one of the holes in the crank.

3 Cut the collet E from dowel.
4 Cut the camshaft F from dowel.
5 Tap and glue the camshaft into the other hole in the crank.

Cutting the blocks, rods and letters

1 Cut nine blocks A on Plan 1 from stripwood. Drill 6mm (0.24in) central holes in their bottom edges to the depth indicated.
2 Cut nine follower rods B on Plan 1 from dowel. Drill 1mm (0.04in) holes in their ends as indicated.
3 Tap and glue their ends into the blocks as indicated.

4 Cut out the nine 'HOLLYWOOD' letters from plywood on Plan 1.

Cutting the cams, fascias and extra bearings bar

1 Cut nine eccentric cams B on Plan 2 from dowels.
2 Drill 8mm (0.32in) holes in them as shown.
3 Cut two fascias A on Plan 4 from battening (PSE).
4 Cut the extra bearings bar B from battening (PSE).
5 Glue the extra bearings bar to the underside of the platform A on Plan 3 using the plan as a guide for positioning.

Detail of the friction block into which the friction rod is inserted. The friction collet on the end of the camshaft spins the friction disc when turned.

6 Drill 7mm (0.28in) holes right through the bearings bar and platform.

7 Turning the platform face upwards, glue the two fascias A on Plan 4 to either side of the holes as shown on A, Plan 3.

Cutting out the friction block assembly

1 Cut out the star G on Plan 2 from plywood. Drill a central 6mm (0.24in) hole between its 'legs', as indicated.

2 Cut the friction disc H from dowel, or plywood if you are not able to obtain dowel at this size.

3 Cut the friction collar I from dowel. Drill a central hole in the collar.

4 Cut out the friction block J from battening (PSE).

5 Drill a central 7mm (0.28in) hole to the depth indicated.

Painting and stencilling

1 Paint the front, sides and back panel dark blue. Do likewise for the friction block assembly, except for its inside edge (which is to be glued) and the crank handle. Don't paint anything inside the box.

2 Paint the star gold all over.

3 Paint the HOLLYWOOD letters white all over, except their bases. Be careful not to reverse them.

4 Glue the letters to the centres of the top edges of the blocks.

5 Paint the blocks on all sides except their bases where the

rods are fixed. Starting at 'H' the block colours are: red, kingfisher blue, emerald green, shocking pink, chrome yellow, mauve, beige, sky blue and bright orange.

6 For stencilling the stars, you need to cut guides from thickened photocopies of the decorated panels on Plans 1 and 4. Spray-glue the reverse sides of the stars and do likewise to two blank A4 sheets. Bond them together and burnish down firmly.

7 Cut out the stars from the (reinforced) front, back and fascia panels. Lightly spray-glue their reverse sides and wait for the glue to dry slightly before gently brushing them by hand onto the areas to be stencilled. You don't want any glue to adhere to the work, so it must be tacky.

8 Using a stiff stencil brush, dab white paint sparingly into the stars. Don't overload the brush or the paint will bleed under the stencil.

9 Gently peel off the stencil and retouch with blue and white paint as necessary.

Assembling the piece

1 Now that all is painted and stencilled the box can be glued and pinned together. Refer to the notes on making boxes (*see* pp12–13). The pinheads should be painted blue.

2 Glue and pin the side panels A on Plan 2 to the base A on Plan 3 and under the platform.

3 Glue and pin the Aeroply front panel to the front edges of the sides, platform and base.

4 Insert the camshaft, with its attached handle, into a side panel bearing, depending on whether right or left hand operation is required.

5 Slide the nine eccentric cams onto the camshaft and insert its end into the other side panel bearing.

6 Arrange the cams as in the illustrations or create your own mobile effect, positioning the cams under their followers. They could be arranged as a controlled wave, but that would seem to be rather mechanical and tame, especially when images of moving piano keys or even Monty Python movable teeth come to mind.

7 Once satisfied with the performance of the letters, superglue the cams to the camshaft all round their edges.

8 Insert miniature panel pins into the holes at the end of the follower rods as indicated on B, Plan 1. These act as end stops to prevent the letters from falling out.

9 Glue the friction collar I onto the end of the camshaft, allowing a bit of play between it and the side panel.

10 Glue the friction disc onto the friction rod 33mm (1.3in) from its end. Drop it into the hole in the friction block and ensure that it turns freely. It should just clear the block, resting on the friction collar which makes it spin round.

11 Finally, glue and pin the back panel to the rear edges of the box and the piece is complete.

This view shows the platform and front fascia.

D: front panel

C: letters

A: blocks

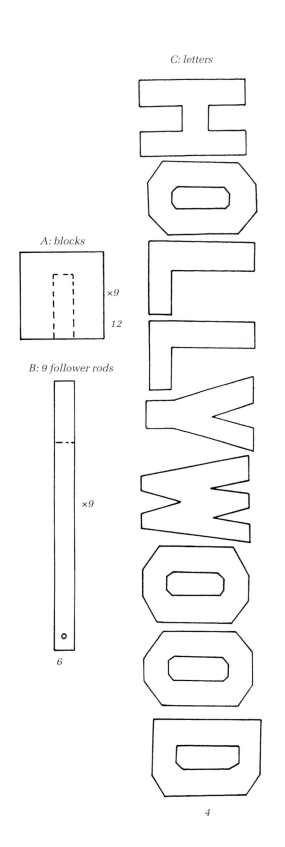

×9

12

B: 9 follower rods

×9

6

4

Plan 1

1.5

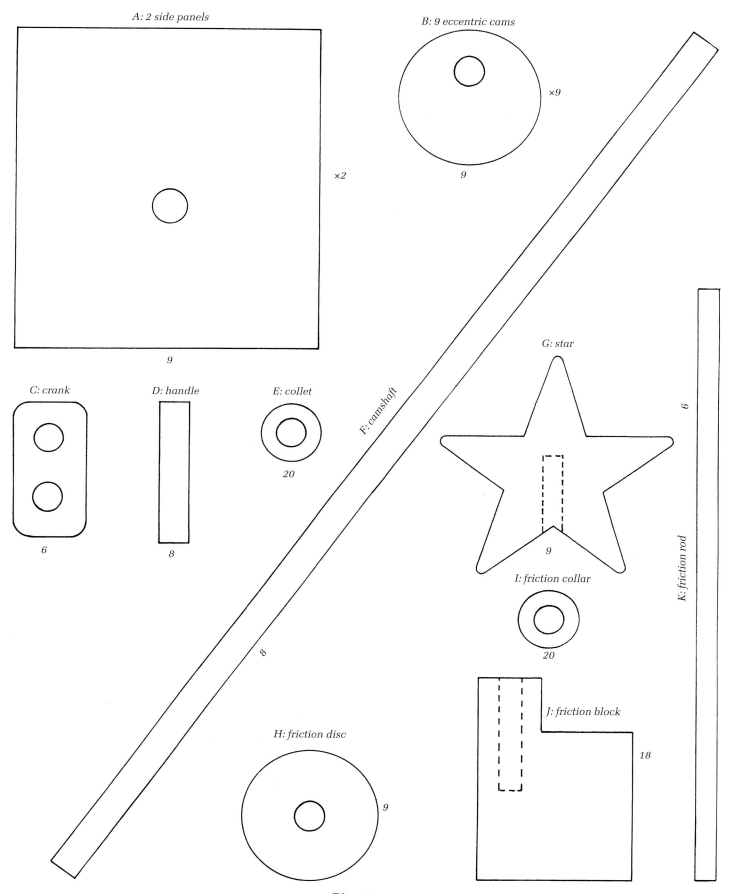

A: 2 side panels
×2
9

B: 9 eccentric cams
×9
9

C: crank
6

D: handle
8

E: collet
20

F: camshaft
8

G: star
9

H: friction disc
9

I: friction collar
20

J: friction block
18

K: friction rod
6

Plan 2

A: platform and base

B: back panel 1st part

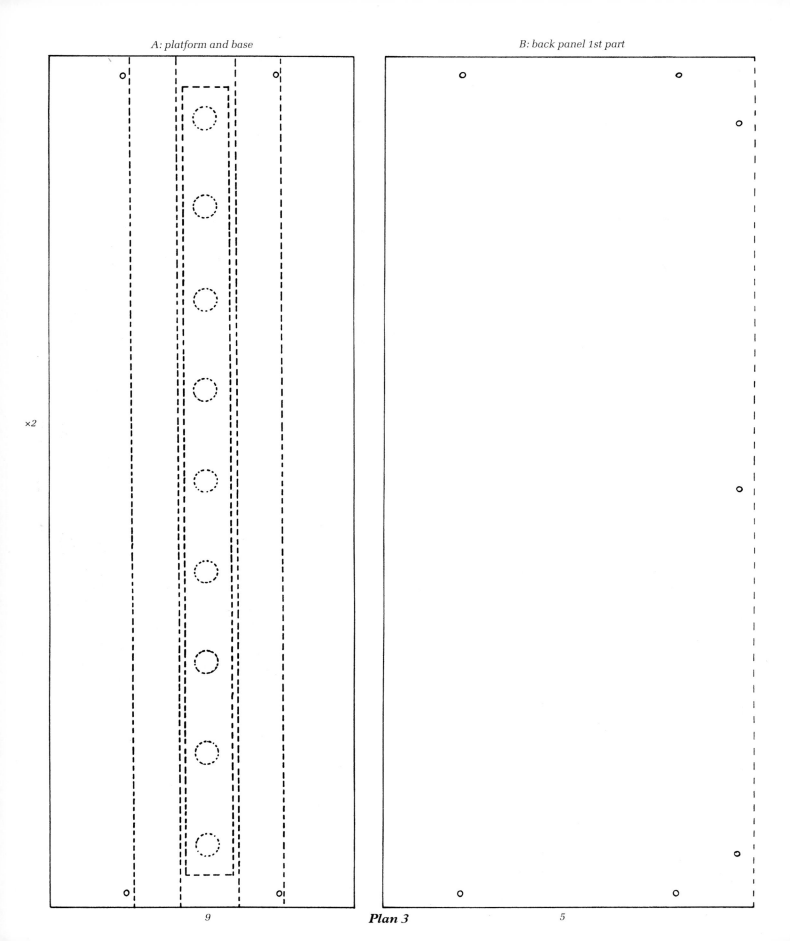

×2

9

Plan 3

5

A: front and rear fascias   B: extra bearings bar

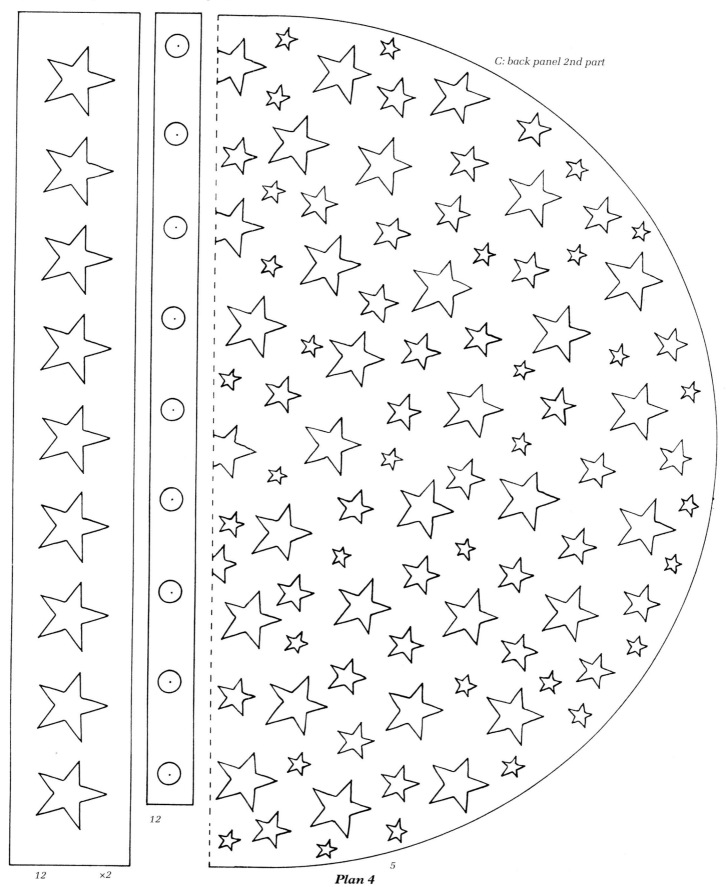

C: back panel 2nd part

12   ×2

12

5

Plan 4

12 MOUSE IN A SPIN

This toy is the harbinger for the next piece: 'MIAOW!', but this is a much simpler piece to construct. It employs the same mechanism as the larger mouse in 'MIAOW!'.

A simple concentric cam spins a friction disc which supports the mouse. He twirls around sniffing the cheese in excitement. A thin piece of polystyrene wall covering glued to the friction disc makes the spinning both more efficient and also quieter.

MATERIALS

PLYWOOD	130 × 137 × 9mm (5.12 × 5.4 × 0.36in)	Side panel, top and bottom panels
AEROPLY	100 × 150 × 1.5mm (3.94 × 5.9 × 0.06in)	Front and back panels, legs and ears
BATTENING (PSE)	37 × 100 × 15mm (1.46 × 3.94 × 0.59in)	Mouse block
STRIPWOOD	17 × 50 × 10mm (0.67 × 1.97 × 0.4in)	Crank
DOWEL	50 × 38mm (1.97 × 1.5in)	Follower disc with polystyrene
	50 × 25mm (1.97 × 0.98in)	Concentric cam
	50 × 16mm (1.97 × 0.63in)	Two collets, end collets
	130 × 8mm (5.12 × 0.32in)	Camshaft, handle
	50 × 5mm (1.97 × 0.20in)	Follower rod
POLYSTYRENE WALL COVERING	50 × 50 × 1mm (1.97 × 1.97 × 0.04in)	

Cutting out the mouse

1 Cut out two legs A and two ears B from Aeroply.
2 Drill a central 5mm (0.20in) hole in the base of the mouse block E to the depth indicated.
3 Drill a 2.5mm (0.1in) hole for the string tail.
4 Cut out the mouse from the block on the continuous line.
5 Cut 2mm (0.08in) thick string 55mm (2.17in) long.

Cutting out the mechanism

1 Cut out the crank C from stripwood. Drill two holes in it as shown.

Mouse in a Spin.
98 × 108 × 67mm (3.86 × 4.26 × 2.64in).

2 Cut out the camshaft D from dowel. Tap and glue it into a hole in the crank.
3 Cut out the handle G from dowel. Tap and glue it into the other hole in the crank.
4 Cut out the concentric cam F from dowel. Drill an 8mm (0.24in) hole in the centre.
5 Cut the follower rod J from dowel. Tap and glue this into the base of the mouse.
6 Cut the follower disc N from dowel or, if unobtainable at this size, cut out from plywood.
7 Glue the disc to a piece of 1mm (0.04in) thick polystyrene with a Pritt Stick or similar adhesive. Many glues dissolve polystyrene, so be careful.
8 Drill a central 5mm (0.20in) hole through the follower disc and its covering. Trim off the waste.

The camshaft handle with the follower disc, mouse and follower rod above the concentric cam flanked by two collets.

The follower rod is glued into the mouse and inserted through the top panel into the follower disc below.

9 Cut out the two collets L from dowel (these are the exterior and interior collets). Drill 8mm (0.24in) holes in them.

10 Slide the exterior collet L along the camshaft and glue it to the crank.

11 For safekeeping slide the interior collet L onto the camshaft, also the concentric cam F and the end collet M.

Cutting out the cheese block

1 Cut out the top and bottom panels, H, from plywood. If possible, cut them both simultaneously by bonding two pieces of plywood together.

2 Drill a central 6mm (0.24in) bearing through the two panels. Drill the cheese holes, with various sized bits, only half way into the top as indicated. Take the panels apart.

3 Cut out the two side panels I together if possible. Drill a central 9mm (0.36in) bearing through both panels.

4 Using a fresh photocopy of side panel I spray-glue it on the back and stick it to the other side panel.

5 Again, drill cheese holes only half way into the side panels, as indicated. Take the panels apart.

6 Cut out, together, the front and back panels K from Aeroply. Drill cheese holes right through both panels as indicated.

7 Glue the side panels I to the top and base panels H as indicated by the dotted lines. Don't pin the panels because so many holes will need to be drilled!

8 Glue the front panel K to the edges of the other panels. Don't fix the back panel until you have installed the mechanism. Sandpaper the box, chamfering the edges.

Painting the parts

1 Paint the mouse's two legs A grey with pink feet as indicated by the dotted lines. Paint the eyes black and white.
2 Paint the body E grey with pink interiors in the ears, as indicated. Paint the mouse's nose and string tail pink.
3 Paint the crank handle and the exterior collet blue.
4 Paint the cheese block yellow mixed with white, and let plenty of paint run into the holes.

Assembling the parts

1 Glue the mouse's legs and ears to his body as indicated.
2 Insert the string tail and glue the end over his back and between his ears.

3 Insert the follower rod J through the hole in the top panel H and into the follower disc N, flush with the polystyrene surface.
4 Remove the two collets and concentric cam which have been safely kept on the camshaft.
5 Insert the camshaft, with its assembled handle, into a side panel, depending on whether you want left or right-hand winding. Fit the interior collet L, the concentric cam F and the end collet M onto the shaft.
6 Glue the interior collet, 1mm (0.04in) away from the side, onto the camshaft.
7 Fix and glue the concentric cam to the shaft so that the follower disc rests on it between its centre and outside edge. (See the illustration.)
8 Glue the end collet M to the camshaft 1mm (0.04in) away from the side, so that there is a little lateral play in the shaft.
9 Glue the back panel to the edges of the other panels. Retouch with yellow paint as necessary.
10 Turn the handle clockwise or anti-clockwise to spin the mouse.

The camshaft is inserted through a side panel and the concentric cam is fitted onto it with a collet either side.

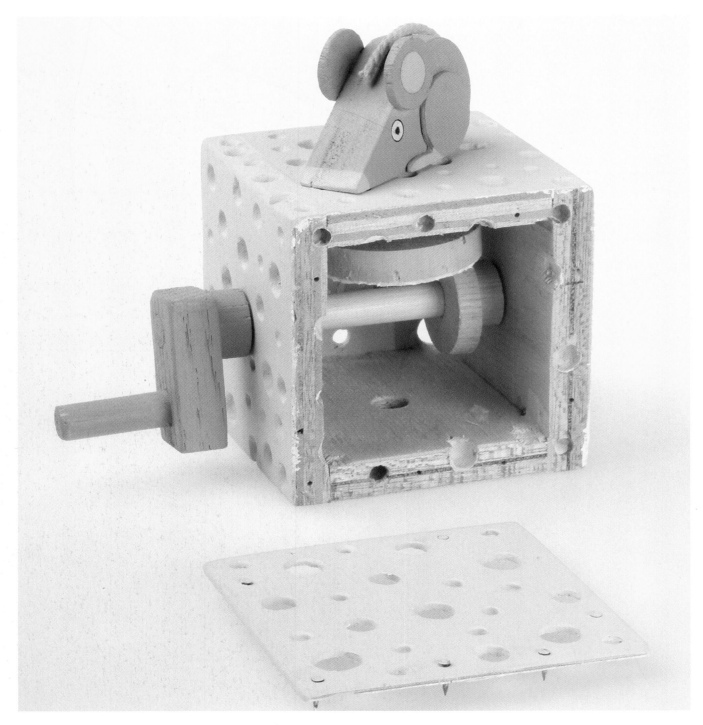

The collets are fixed at either end of the camshaft with the follower disc resting on the concentric cam. The Aeroply back panel is then glued into position.

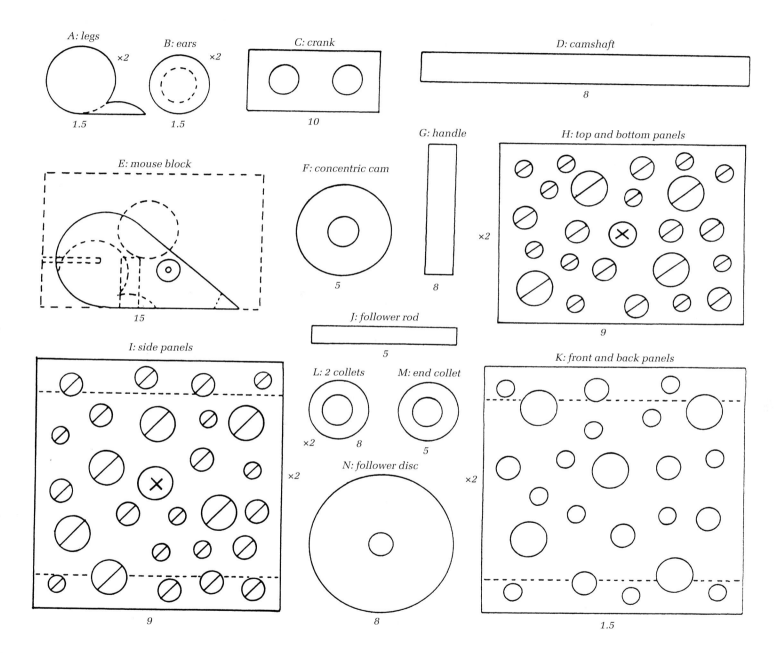

A: legs ×2
1.5

B: ears ×2
1.5

C: crank
10

D: camshaft
8

E: mouse block
15

F: concentric cam
5

G: handle
8

H: top and bottom panels ×2
9

I: side panels ×2
9

J: follower rod
5

L: 2 collets ×2
8

M: end collet
5

N: follower disc
8

K: front and back panels ×2
1.5

13 MIAOW!

This is probably the most complex piece to make in the book, with six plans and lots of fiddly little pieces to cut out and lose. Always keep bags or tins available to store any adventurous little components.

Originally, the piece was called 'Cat and Mouse' until a gap was found in the design to allow for the addition of the larger mouse. He spins round in a circular frenzy while the smaller mouse, trying to get at the cheese, twists and turns evading the paw which is repeatedly thrust out by the cat.

Mechanically, the main elements are two friction discs and a piston rod. A concentric cam turns the mouse's follower friction disc which spins the larger mouse. The end of the camshaft is fixed to a large wheel which operates a piston and a vertical rod. At the top of the rod, a string loop links the sliding action of the piston block to the eyes slider panel. This allows the cat's eyes to flick from side to side.

Down below, the piston block, which houses the rod and friction follower disc of the little mouse, moves it laterally within a slot. The friction disc, oscillating on a friction bar, produces a scuttling performance from the little mouse.

A string attached to the cat's foot, looped around its ear and attached to the piston wheel, lifts the leg ensuring that it just misses the little mouse on every revolution. It works clockwise or anti-clockwise.

MATERIALS

PLYWOOD	407 × 280 × 9mm (16.03 × 11.02 × 0.36in)	Thick cat, platform, bearings, box top, bottom and side panels
	160 × 170 × 3mm (6.3 × 6.69 × 0.12in)	Medium cat
	110 × 110 × 5mm (4.34 × 4.34 × 0.20in)	Piston wheel
AEROPLY	432 × 260 × 1.5mm (17.01 × 10.23 × 0.06in)	Thin cat, mice legs and ears, bearings, box front and back, end panel, eyes slider, nose
BATTENING (PSE)	80 × 320 × 20mm (3.15 × 12.6 × 0.79in)	Front and end panels, cheese, piston, block and slider
	43 × 190 × 15mm (1.7 × 7.48 × 0.59in)	Rear panel, part 1
	15 × 190 × 15mm (0.59 × 7.48 × 0.59in)	Friction bar
	37 × 80 × 15mm (1.46 × 3.15 × 0.59in)	First mouse block
	25 × 60 × 18mm (0.98 × 2.36 × 0.71in)	Support block
	30 × 60 × 12mm (1.18 × 2.36 × 0.47in)	Second mouse block
STRIPWOOD	10 × 100 × 10mm (0.4 × 3.94 × 0.4in)	Two corner supports
	16 × 60 × 10mm (0.63 × 2.36 × 0.4in)	Crank
	43 × 170 × 5mm (1.7 × 6.7 × 0.20in)	Rear panel, part 2
	14 × 140 × 3mm (0.55 × 5.52 × 0.12in)	Piston rod

continued

MIAOW!
209 × 245 × 191mm (8.23 × 9.64 × 7.52in).

MATERIALS *continued*

Stripwood (*cont.*)	12 × 110 × 3mm (0.47 × 4.34 × 0.12in)	Vertical rod
	15 × 35 × 3mm (0.59 × 1.38 × 0.12in)	Support bar
	8 × 330 × 1mm (0.32 × 12.99 × 0.04in)	Four guide rails
	22 × 190 × 3mm (0.87 × 7.48 × 0.12in)	Platform extension
Dowel	38 × 80mm (1.5 × 3.15in)	Four discs
	19 × 60mm (0.75 × 2.36in)	Three collets
	200 × 8mm (7.87 × 0.32in)	Camshaft, handle, eyes slider pin
	210 × 6mm (8.27 × 0.24in)	Two mouse rods, piston slider pin, wheel pin, vertical rod pin
Elastic band (cut)	6 × 180 × 1mm (0.24 × 7.09 × 0.04in)	
Polystyrene wall covering	45 × 30 × 1mm (1.77 × 1.18 × 0.04in)	
Pink card	20 × 50 × 1mm (0.79 × 1.97 × 0.04in)	

Cutting out the cat

1 Cut out three different thicknesses of the body from 180 × 160mm (7.09 × 6.3in) sheets: 9mm (0.36in) and 3mm (0.12in) in plywood and 1.5mm (0.06in) Aeroply.

2 Temporarily bond the pieces together. Cut out three cats from D on Plan 1.

3 Cut out the left front leg as indicated. Drill a central 2mm (0.08in) hole at the top, through its side, indicated by the dotted lines.

4 Take the three sections of the leg apart and glue them all together. Keep a 2mm drill bit in the hole to ensure exact fit.

5 Cut out the slot in the fattest cat as indicated by the shaded area on A Plan 1.

6 Cut out the complete slot, from head to tail, in the medium thickness cat.

7 Drill two 12mm (0.47in) eye holes in the thinnest cat.

8 Remove the 2mm drill bit from the cat's leg and cut out the inverted 'U' joint.

9 Cut a panel pin flush with the leg and insert it through the joint.

10 Shape the upright part of the joint into a curve, as indicated, so that the paw almost reaches the ground. This will necessitate shaving off some of the paw. It must be possible for the leg to be raised parallel to the ground and to stop just clear of it when lowered. Test the leg movement with the pin in place. Keep the jointed leg safely until you glue it to the body.

Making the eyes slider

1 Cut out the eyes slider E on Plan 2 from Aeroply.

2 Cut the blink panel G from pink card.

3 Cut the eyes slider pin F from dowel. Drill a 1mm (0.04in) hole in the top as shown.

4 Drill an 8mm (0.32in) hole in the unshaded circle on the eyes slider.

5 Tap and glue the eyes slider pin F into the eyes slider.

Assembling and painting the cat

1 Paint the eyes slider E on Plan 2 white and the two shaded circles black.

2 Assemble the three cat sections in the order in which you cut them.

3 Glue the blink panel G on Plan 2 to the rear, thickest, section of the cat behind the eye holes on Plan 1.

4 Insert the eyes slider pin F into the smaller slot in the rear section. The eyes slider itself rests in the channel of the middle section slot.

5 Glue the rear and middle sections of the cat together.

6 Paint the rims of the eyes orange.

7 Glue the front Aeroply section to the glued sections.

8 Prime the cat with matt (vinyl) white emulsion. Work carefully around the eyes and ensure you do not impair the leg movement, which is not yet fixed.

9 Paint the cat orange all over. Again, be careful around the eyes and do not clog the jointed leg. Test it now and glue it in position to the body.

10 Cut out a photocopy of the cat stencil K on Plan 2. Spray-glue it to a sheet of paper and burnish thoroughly. Cut around the stencil leaving an ample border. Now, cut out the triangles.

11 Lightly spray the back of the cut stencil. Place it gently in position over the cat.

12 With a stiff stencil brush dab tan paint into the stripes. Use pink for the ears. Remove the stencil.

13 Paint tan coloured stripes on the side edges of the cat continuing the triangles.

14 Using a broad black fibre-tipped pen, draw the mouth with the aid of a coin or a circles template.

15 Cut out the nose E on Plan 1 and colour it pink.

16 Glue the nose as indicated by the plan.

17 Use diluted orange paint to stain a piece of thin string (150mm (5.9in) long). When dry, thread it through the hole in the paw and tie a knot at the back.

Making the bearings box

1 Cut out the top and bottom panels C on Plan 4 from plywood. Cut them simultaneously if possible by temporarily bonding two pieces of plywood, and then take them apart.

2 Drill a central 7mm (0.28in) hole in the top panel.

3 Cut out the two side panels G from plywood, together.

4 Drill 9mm (0.36in) bearings through the two panels. Take them apart.

5 Cut out the front and back panels H, together, from Aeroply.

6 Glue and pin the top and bottom panels between the side panels. Refer to the notes on making boxes (see pp12–13).

7 Glue and pin the front panel to the edges of the other panels. Leave the back open until the end.

Making the bearings box mechanism

1 Cut the camshaft E on Plan 3 from dowel.

2 Cut the crank F from stripwood. Drill 8mm (0.32in) holes at either end.

3 Cut the handle L from dowel. Tap and glue it into the crank.

4 Tap and glue the camshaft into the other hole in the crank.

5 Cut the handle collet N from dowel. Drill an 8mm (0.32in) hole in it. Slide it onto the camshaft and glue it next to the crank.

6 Cut the concentric cam H on Plan 2 from dowel. Drill a central 8mm (0.32in) hole in it.

7 Cut the first mouse follower disc D from dowel.

8 With a Pritt stick (or similar adhesive), glue 1mm (0.04in) polystyrene wall covering to the first mouse follower D. Cut away the waste.

9 Drill a 6mm (0.24in) central hole in the follower disc D.

10 Cut the first mouse rod C from dowel.

11 Tap and friction-fit the rod into the follower disc with the polystyrene covering.

12 Insert the other end of the rod, from below, into the hole in the underside of the top panel. Hold it there while you insert the camshaft into the bearings box.

13 Slide the concentric cam H on Plan 2 onto the shaft, positioning it under the outer edge of the follower disc with the polystyrene covering. Let the camshaft rest in its bearings.

Cutting out the piston assembly

1 Cut out the piston wheel B on Plan 3 from plywood.

2 Drill a central 8mm (0.32in) hole in it. Drill a 6mm (0.24in) hole in the outer edge.

3 Cut out the piston rod O from stripwood.

4 Drill 8mm (0.32in) holes at both ends of the rod.

5 Cut the vertical rod D from stripwood.

The bearings box interior shows the camshaft with a concentric cam supporting the outer edge of the mouse follower disc.

6 Drill 6mm (0.24in) holes at both ends of the rod.
7 Cut out the piston disc B on Plan 4. Drill a central 6mm (0.24in) hole.
8 Cut the wheel pin D from dowel.
9 Cut the piston disc collet E from dowel. Drill a 6mm (0.24in) hole.
10 Cut the vertical rod collet F from dowel. Drill a 6mm (0.24in) hole.

Assembling the piston components

1 Friction-fit the piston wheel B on Plan 3 to the end of the protruding camshaft. Ensure there is a 2mm (0.08in) gap between the wheel and side panel.
2 Tap and glue the wheel pin D on Plan 4 into the hole on the outer edge of the piston wheel, flush with it.
3 Place the piston rod O on Plan 3 onto the wheel pin.
4 Friction-fit the piston disc B on Plan 4 onto the pin leaving enough room for the piston rod to move freely.
5 Glue the piston collet E to the end of the wheel pin.

Cutting out the platform

1 Cut the front panel A on Plan 5 from battening.
2 Cut two guide rails B from stripwood.
3 Cut the platform extension C from stripwood.
4 Glue the two guide rails to the edges of the platform extension shown by the dotted lines, flush with the top of it, so that they hang down.
5 Cut out the platform D from plywood.
6 Cut out the interior slot as indicated.
7 Cut the friction bar I on Plan 4 from battening. Glue it to the inside of the front panel A on Plan 5 as shown by the dotted lines.
8 Glue a wide elastic band A on Plan 3 on top of the bar.
9 Cut two more guide rails B on Plan 6 from stripwood.
10 Cut out part 1 of the rear panel C on Plan 6 from battening.
11 Cut out part 2 of the rear panel D from stripwood. Glue this to part 1, flush with the right end of the panel, as indicated by the dotted lines.
12 Glue the two guide rails B to either side of the glued panels so that a third protrudes above the edges forming a channel, as indicated by the dotted lines.
13 Cut out the end panel support G on Plan 3 from plywood.
14 Cut out the end panel M from Aeroply. Draw your own profile shape once the platform D on Plan 5 has been assembled (*see* below).

Assembling the platform

1 Glue the platform extension C on Plan 5, with its guide rails, flush with the top edge of the platform.
2 Glue the end panel support G on Plan 3 between the lower parts of the front and back panels, under the friction bar at the front and a guide rail at the back.
3 Glue and pin the platform D on Plan 5 onto the front panel and end support panel G on Plan 3.
4 Insert the little support bar B on Plan 2 gluing the bottom to the top of the back panel, or channel, and the top of the bar to the underside of the platform extension C on Plan 5, indicated by the vertical dotted line.
5 Now, glue the ends of the front and back panels and the back of the support bar to the front of the bearings box. Ensure all is square.
6 Glue the corner supports A on Plan 4 under the friction bar at either end of the inside of the rear panel.

Making the interior mechanism

1 Cut out the piston block slider L on Plan 2 from battening. Drill a 7mm (0.28in) hole in the top of the block, as indicated.
2 Cut the piston block O from battening. Drill a central 6mm (0.24in) hole.
3 Cut the piston slider pin P from dowel.
4 Tap and glue the piston slider pin into the piston block flush with its end.
5 Glue the small rectangle on the piston block slider to the piston block as indicated by the dotted lines.
6 Slide the piston block assembly into the channel, between the top and bottom guide rails. Check that it runs smoothly.
7 Cut the vertical rod pin M from dowel. Drill a 1mm (0.04in) hole into the end as indicated.
8 Tap and glue the pin into the vertical rod D on Plan 3 so that the holes face East-West.
9 Cut the support block A on Plan 2 from battening. Glue it on the corner, in the channel, flush with the end of the back panel.

Assembling the vertical rod components

1 Place the piston rod O on Plan 3 onto the piston slider pin P on Plan 2.
2 Glue the vertical rod D on Plan 3, with its pin, to the end of the piston slider pin and its collet F on Plan 4. Ensure it is perpendicular.
3 Thread thin string through the pin at the top of the vertical rod and the eyes slider pin.

ABOVE: An interior view shows a corner support, the friction bar, the piston block slider, the 2nd mouse's follower disc and the slotted channel in the platform.

ABOVE RIGHT: Detail of the friction bar and the 2nd mouse's follower disc, the outer edge of which rests upon it. The piston block slider, beneath, is glued to the piston block which slides along a channel.

RIGHT: The shaping of the end panel to accommodate the various projections is shown here. The support block, on the corner, is glued in the channel once the piston block slider assembly is installed.

4   Experiment by tying a knot in the loop so that the eyes slider operates correctly: eyes swivelling laterally with an interval for a pink blink.

Cutting out the mice components

1   The first mouse's follower disc with the polystyrene covering is resting, with its rod, on the concentric cam within the bearings box. Now cut the second mouse's follower disc J on Plan 3 from dowel. Roughen one surface by scratching cross-hatched cuts over it.
2   Drill a 6mm (0.24in) central hole in the follower disc J.
3   Cut the second mouse rod H from dowel.
4   Tap and friction-fit the rod into the follower disc J.

5 Cut out the cheese B and C on Plan 1 from battening.

6 Drill holes through the sides C as indicated.

Cutting out the mice

1 Cut out the first mouse's two legs I on Plan 2 from Aeroply.

2 Cut out the second mouse's two legs I on Plan 3 from Aeroply.

3 Cut out the first mouse's ears J on Plan 2 from dowel.

4 Cut out the second mouse's ears K on Plan 3 from dowel.

5 Drill a central 6mm (0.24in) hole in the base of the first mouse block N on Plan 2. Do likewise for the second mouse block C on Plan 3, to the depths indicated.

6 Drill 2.5mm (0.1in) holes for the string tails in both mice.

7 Cut out the mice from the blocks.

8 Cut 2mm (0.08in) thick string 55 mm (2.17in) long.

9 Remove the first mouse follower disc, with its polystyrene covering and rod, from the bearings box. Just withdraw the camshaft which is friction-fitted to the piston wheel.

10 Withdraw the rod from the follower disc (which was only friction-fitted). Tap and glue it into the underside of the first mouse, as indicated.

11 Tap and glue the second mouse rod H on Plan 3 into the underside of the second mouse.

Priming, painting and stencilling

1 Refer to the notes on painting. Prime the parts to be painted with matt (vinyl) white emulsion.

2 Paint the platform and bearings box Indian yellow. Paint the handle and crank blue and the collet Indian yellow.

3 Cut out a copy of the MIAOW! stencil A on Plan 6. Before cutting out the rectangle and letters, spray-glue the stencil to a sheet of paper to strengthen it.

4 Lightly spray the back of the stencil and place it gently over the front panel.

5 With a stiff stencil brush dab blue paint into the letters. Remove the stencil.

6 Paint the mice and their legs and ears grey. Paint noses, tails, feet and inside the ears pink as indicated by the dotted lines on Plans 2 and 3. The eyes in black and white are best drawn with the aid of a circles template and a fine black fibre-tipped pen.

7 Glue the tails, legs and ears to the mice as indicated by the dotted lines.

Fixing the mice

1 Insert the first mouse's rod through the top of the bearings box and into the follower disc with the polystyrene cover, and then reposition the camshaft in its bearing. The outside edge of the disc rests on the concentric cam on the camshaft. Test the action of the mouse, which must be off the ground.

2 When satisfied, glue the concentric cam to the shaft and the piston wheel to the end of the camshaft.

3 Tap and glue the back panel H on Plan 4 to the edges of the top, bottom and side panels.

4 Place the second mouse's follower disc J on Plan 3 between the friction bar and its rubber band and the underside of the platform. Hold it there.

5 Insert the second mouse's rod through the slot in the platform and the follower disc into the piston block slider L on Plan 2.

6 The friction disc's roughened edge rests on the elastic band (glued to the friction bar). The disc should be positioned between the underside of the platform slot and the piston block slider below.

7 Ensure that the small mouse does not touch the surface and can twirl quite freely.

Fixing the cat

1 Glue the cat's three static legs to the platform and the side of the front leg to the front panel of the bearings box. Ensure that all is square and that the cat's leg lines up with the edge of the front panel, clear of the piston wheel. Check that the movable leg can rise parallel to the platform.

2 Thread thin string through the holes in the eyes slider pin and the vertical rod pin. (*See* the illustration.) Tie a knot which allows the eyes slider to function.

3 Place the orange string, attached to the cat's paw, around the cat's right ear and tie it in a wide loop (not too tightly) around the piston wheel pin with the piston extended to the left, as you look at the back of the piece.

4 Looking from the front, the leg is raised, the eyes look right and the little mouse is at the bearings box end of his run.

5 Turn the crank and the string goes limp, the leg drops and the eyes show a pink blink, while the little mouse is now by the cheese.

6 Clockwise or anti-clockwise, the cat misses the mouse with his paw every time!

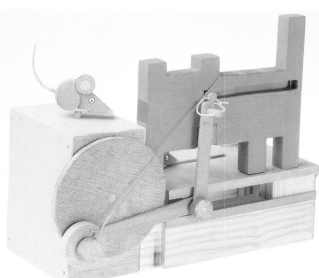

ABOVE LEFT: The legs, ears and tail are painted separately and then glued to the painted body.

ABOVE RIGHT: The piston, extended to the right with the loop attached to the vertical bar, is linked to the eyes slider.

LEFT: The piston, extended to the left, pulls the eyes slider to the left.

BELOW LEFT: The larger mouse continuously twirls around, watched by the cat.

BELOW RIGHT: As the smaller mouse moves to the cheese, the cat's eyes blink pink.

A: eyes slider panel

C: cheese sides

B: cheese top

×2

E: nose

1.5

20

D: cutter guide for 3 thicknesses of cat

×3   9, 3, 1.5

Plan 1

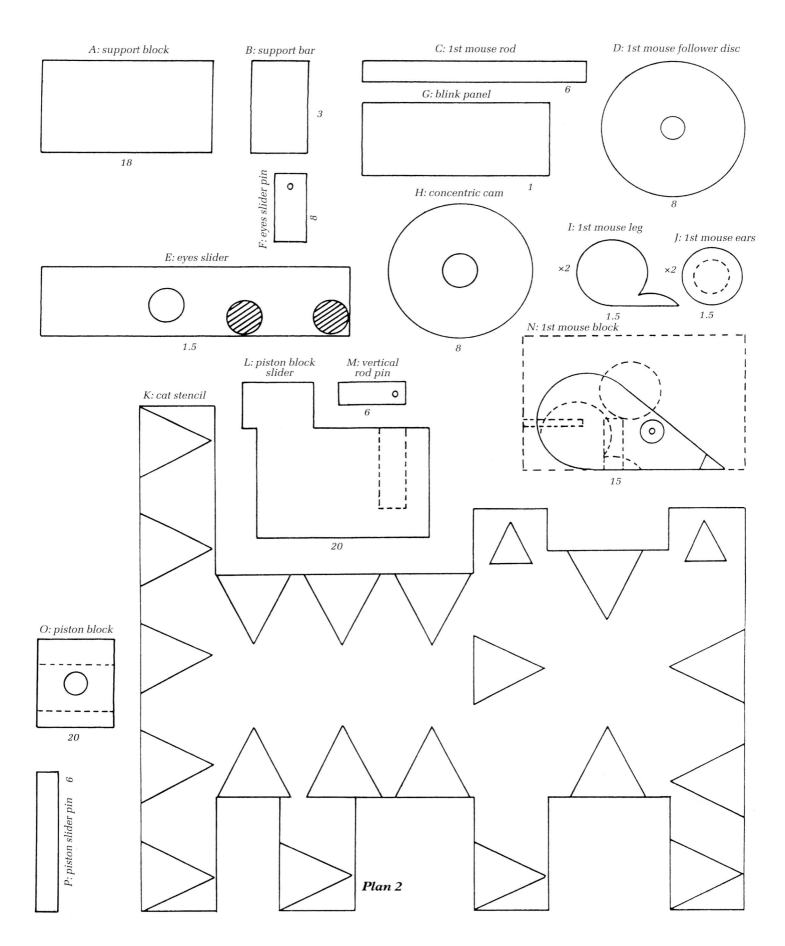

A: support block
18

B: support bar
3

C: 1st mouse rod
6

D: 1st mouse follower disc
8

G: blink panel
1

F: eyes slider pin
8

H: concentric cam
8

E: eyes slider
1.5

I: 1st mouse leg
×2
1.5

J: 1st mouse ears
×2
1.5

N: 1st mouse block
15

L: piston block slider

M: vertical rod pin
6

K: cat stencil

20

O: piston block
20

P: piston slider pin
6

Plan 2

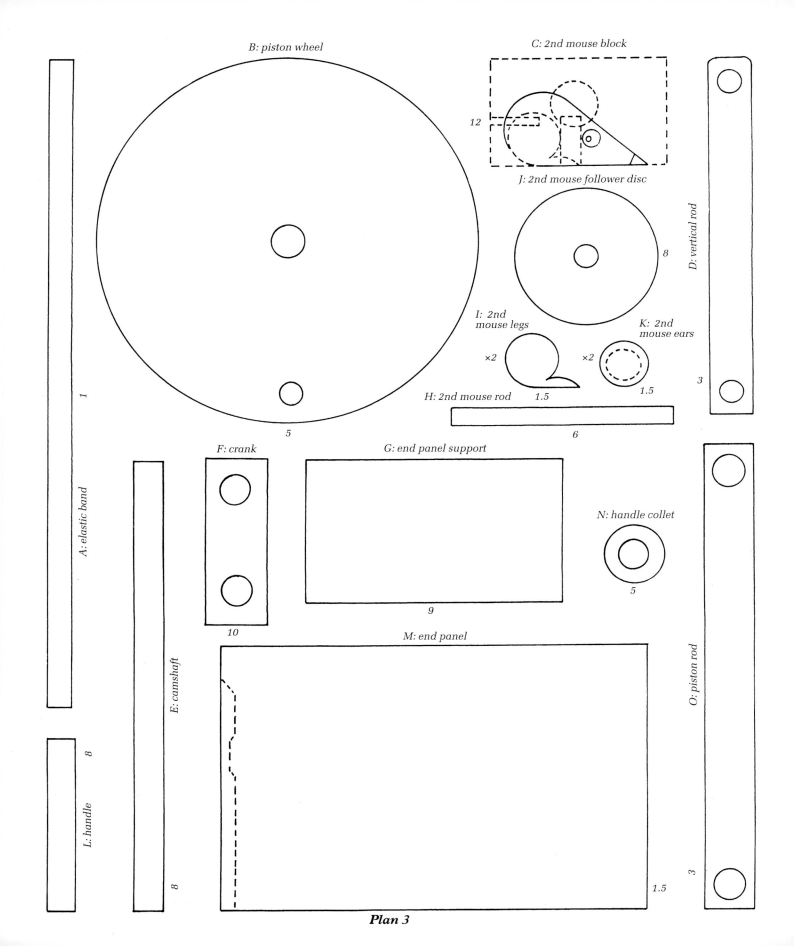

B: piston wheel

C: 2nd mouse block

12

J: 2nd mouse follower disc

8

D: vertical rod

I: 2nd mouse legs

K: 2nd mouse ears

×2

×2

H: 2nd mouse rod

1.5

1.5

3

1

5

6

A: elastic band

F: crank

G: end panel support

N: handle collet

10

9

5

E: camshaft

M: end panel

O: piston rod

L: handle

8

8

3

1.5

Plan 3

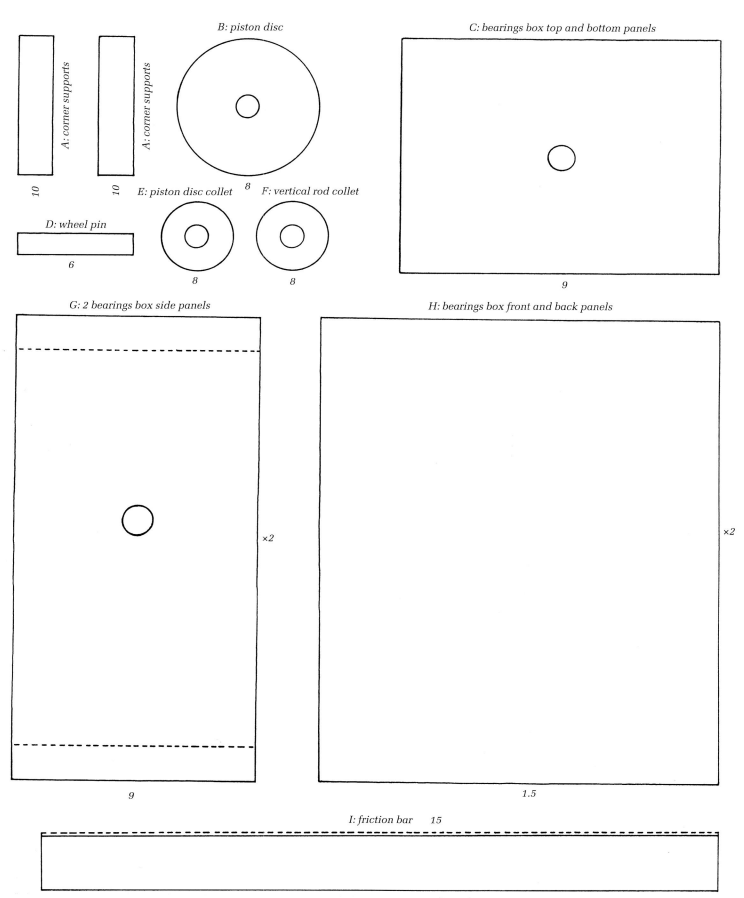

Plan 4

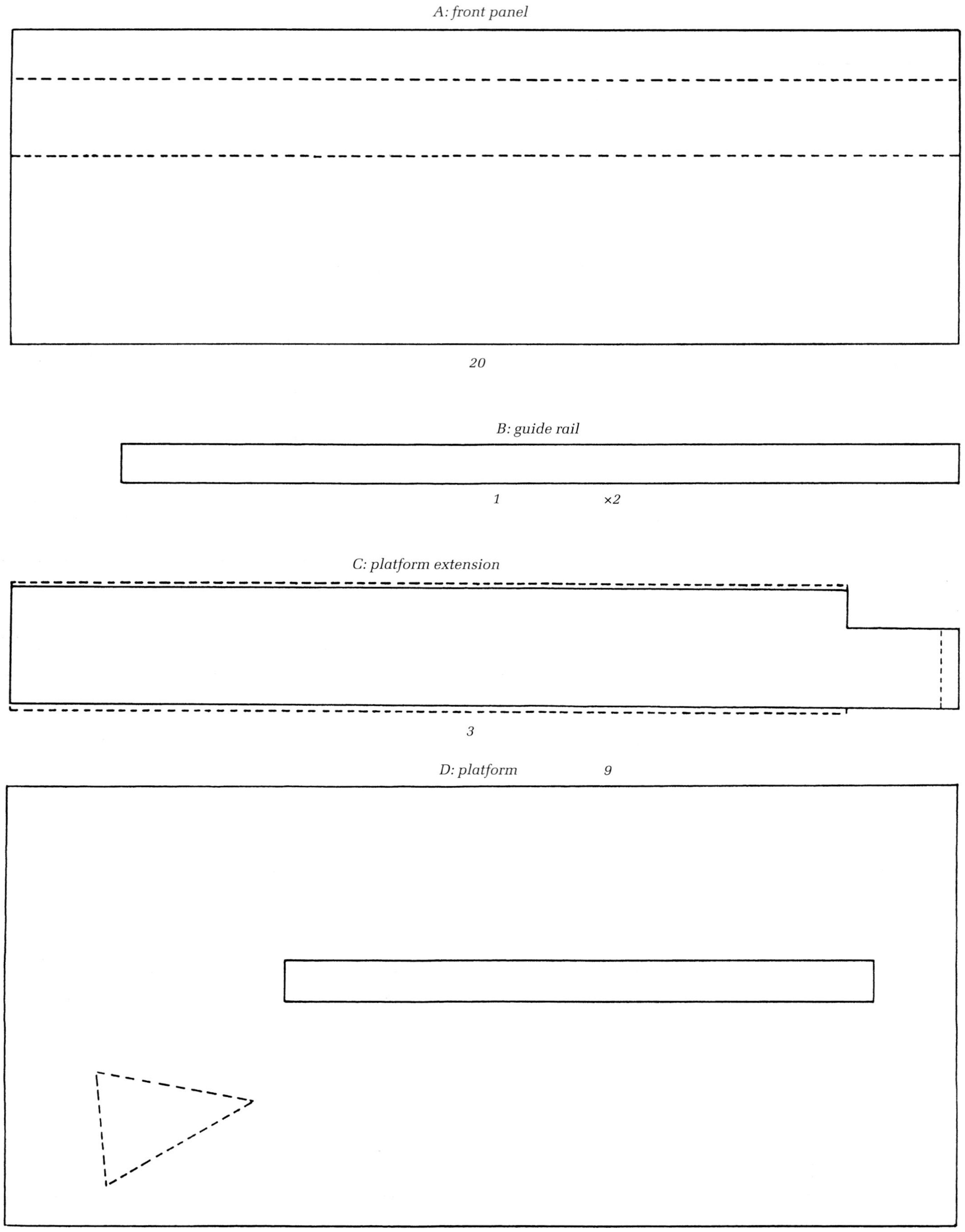

A: front panel

20

B: guide rail

1   ×2

C: platform extension

3

D: platform   9

Plan 5

A: MIAOW! stencil

B: 2nd guide rail

1   ×2

C: rear panel (part 1)

15

D: rear panel (part 2)

5

Plan 6

14 BOAT AND THREE FISH

Sometimes the inspiration for a piece can come from seeing or reading about the mechanics of an automaton. Such was the case with this toy, which has its genesis in an eighteenth-century beauty-spot box. It contained a seascape with a ship moving up and down with three waves arranged in depth, giving a very realistic illusion of a rough sea.

This modern version employs the same mechanism, turning a disc anti-clockwise which turns an adjacent disc clockwise. Three sets of waves are started up, each of which displays a fish. The front waves are attached to revolving cogwheels and a third wave between them, which produces an oscillating motion. The boat, linked to this mechanism, dips and rises an impressive 87mm (3.43in). Because of the accuracy demanded in making the pinwheels it is a fairly difficult piece to make, although ultimately rewarding (but perhaps not for the sea-sick!). Bon Voyage!

MATERIALS

PLYWOOD	250 × 400 × 9mm (9.84 × 15.75 × 0.36in)	Front and back panels
	408 × 210 × 5mm (16.07 × 8.27 × 0.20in)	Two side panels, two cogwheels, two pinwheels
AEROPLY	435 × 309 × 1.5mm (17.14 × 12.17 × 0.06in)	Boat, three waves, sea panel and top
STRIPWOOD	250 × 9 × 6mm (9.84 × 0.36 × 0.24in)	Sea panel supports
	50 × 18 × 8mm (1.97 × 0.71 × 0.32in)	Crank
DOWEL	50 × 8mm (1.97 × 0.31in)	Crankshaft, handle, arbors

Six pop rivets
Masking tape 10mm (0.4in) wide
Fifty panel pins 30mm (1.18in) long

Cutting out the panels

1 Cut out the front and back panels (the full page outline on Plan 1) from plywood. Cut them simultaneously if possible, by temporarily bonding together two panels, then take them apart.
2 Drill two 9mm (0.36in) holes in the front panel as indicated by the cogwheels.
3 Cut out the sea panel A on Plan 4 from Aeroply.
4 Cut out the top panel C on Plan 3 from Aeroply.

Boat and Three Fish.
236 × 188 × 85mm (9.79 × 7.4 × 3.35in).

5 Cut out the two side panels E, simultaneously if possible. Drill a 9mm (0.36in) bearing through both panels.

Cutting out the boat and waves

1 Cut out the boat A on Plan 2 from Aeroply.
2 Drill two 2mm (0.08in) holes in the keel of the boat.
3 Cut out the first wave D, the second wave C and the third wave B, all from Aeroply.
4 Drill two 2mm (0.08in) holes, as indicated, in the first wave D; two holes in the second wave C and three holes in the third wave B.

Cutting the cogwheels and making the pinwheels

1 Cut the cogwheels G and D on Plan 4 from plywood.
2 Drill 8mm (0.32in) central holes in them. Drill 2mm (0.08in) holes at their outer edges as indicated.
3 Cut out the small pinwheel H from plywood.
4 Cut out the large pinwheel I from plywood.
5 Drill central 8mm (0.32in) holes in both pinwheels.
6 Drill twelve 1.5mm (0.06in) holes in the small pinwheel as indicated (*see* comments below).
7 Drill thirty-six 1.5mm (0.06in) holes, as indicated, in the large pinwheel. It is important that these holes are drilled accurately and the use of a pillar drill or drill stand for your electric drill is strongly recommended.
8 Tap 30mm (1.18in) long panel pins into all the holes but one, of each pinwheel. The gaps allow you to fit the nose of your snips into the circle of pins. Cut the panel pins 11mm (0.43in) above the surface of each wheel.
9 Insert the remaining two pins and snip them to the same length as the other pins.
10 Wrap a length of 10mm (0.4in) masking tape around each circle of pins. File off the tops of the pins with the aid of a belt, or circular, sander so that they are level with the tapes. Remove the tapes and you have two circles of pins at a uniform height of 10mm (0.4in).

Cutting out the crankshaft assembly

1 Cut out the crankshaft A on Plan 3 from dowel.
2 Cut the handle F from dowel.
3 Cut the crank G from stripwood. Drill two 8mm (0.32in) holes, as indicated.

The large and small pinwheels have diameters of 20mm (0.79in) and 60mm (2.36in), a 1:3 ratio. The actual sizes of the wheels are slightly larger than the pitch circles upon which the pins are positioned.

4 Cut an exterior and interior handle collet H from dowel (keep one handle collet safely for later; the other will be used soon).

Assembling the crankshaft components

1 Tap and glue the crankshaft A on Plan 3 into the crank G.
2 Tap and glue the handle F into the other hole in the crank.
3 Slide the exterior handle collet H onto the crankshaft and glue it next to the crank.

Cutting and gluing supports, arbors and collets.

1 Cut the sea panel supports B and D on Plan 3 from stripwood.
2 Glue the sea panel supports to the back of the sea panel A on Plan 4, at either end, as indicated by the dotted lines.
3 Cut the two arbors I on Plan 3 from dowel.
4 Tap and glue the arbors into the cogwheels G and D on Plan 4.
5 Cut two exterior arbor washers B and C from dowel (keep these safely to go under the cogwheel).
6 Cut an interior arbor collet E from dowel (keep this safely with the washers).

Priming, painting and sponging

1 Prime the parts to be painted by referring to the colour illustrations, with matt (vinyl) white emulsion. Don't paint the mechanisms.
2 Paint the handle (but not the crankshaft), the crank and the exterior collet, beige.
3 Paint the sides, top panel and their edges, beige.
4 Paint the front panel a gradated blue, darker at the top.
5 Match the inside strips on either side panel to the gradated blue front panel.
6 Sponge liquid blue paint onto the primed white sea panel A on Plan 4 to get a watery, sparkling, effect. Do likewise to the waves B, C and D on Plan 2. They will tend to bow when dry, and to counteract this, paint water on the undersides.
7 Refer to the notes on transferring drawings (*see* p.11). Transfer the drawing of the boat A on Plan 2 onto the primed Aeroply cut-out of the boat A on Plan 2. Burnish it down thoroughly.
8 Paint the boat by referring to the colour illustrations.
9 Transfer the drawings of the fish onto the waves B, C

and D, the primed and sponged cut-outs. Burnish them down thoroughly.

10 Paint the fish on the waves referring to the colour illustrations.

Assembling the box frame and small pinwheel

1 Pin and glue the side panels E on Plan 3 to the front and back panels A on Plan 1, as indicated by the dotted lines on E Plan 3.

2 Insert the crankshaft through the bearing in the right-hand side panel E, ensuring it turns freely within it after painting.

3 Slide the interior handle collet H on Plan 3 (which you have been keeping safely) and position it near the handle end of the crankshaft.

4 Slide the small pinwheel H on Plan 4 onto the crankshaft and then insert the crankshaft into the other bearing.

5 Now, move both the components along the shaft so that the interior handle collet almost touches the inside of the side panel and the pinwheel is 8mm (0.32in) away from it.

6 Ensure the crankshaft can turn freely in its bearings.

Assembling the boat and waves

1 Six pop rivets B on Plan 1 need to be converted to make fixings for the waves and boat. With the aid of pliers and a hammer, tap the sliding parts of the rivets until they come loose. Remove them from the rivet pins but keep them handy.

2 Insert the four 'naked' pins through the four holes in the first and second waves D and C on Plan 2.

3 Insert the lower pins in the waves D and C into the outer holes in the cogwheels D and G on Plan 4.

4 Insert a rivet pin through the centre hole of the third wave B on Plan 2.

5 Insert a rivet pin through the left hand hole in the keel of the boat A.

6 Insert two upper pins in the first and second waves D and C through the two outer holes in the third wave B.

7 Place the waves assembly face down and slide four of the sliding detached parts back onto the rivet pins, but now inverted.

8 Push the inverted parts up against the cogs and the third wave, but not too tightly. Ensure there is ample freedom of movement.

9 Snip off the four inverted parts and superglue the

joints vertically so that the glue runs into the joint but not into the work.

10 Glue two exterior arbor washers B and C on Plan 4 onto the arbors of the cogwheels and their undersides.

Fixing more rivet joints and arbors

1 Insert the central rivet pin in the third wave B on Plan 2 through the right-hand hole in the keel of the boat.

2 Slide one of the two remaining parts of the rivet pins back onto the central pin, but now inverted, like the others. (The other sliding part will not be needed as it will be replaced by the interior boat collet F on Plan 4.)

3 Push the inverted part up against the underside of the boat allowing a 2mm (0.08in) gap between the third wave and the boat.

4 Snip off the inverted part and superglue it as you did with the other joints.

5 Insert the two cogwheel arbors (with washers attached) into the holes in the front panel. At the same time, insert the rivet pin in the keel into the hole indicated by the black dot on the keel on Plan 1.

Fixing collets and large pinwheel

1 From inside the box frame, place the interior boat collet F on Plan 4 onto the protruding rivet pin. Allowing a 3mm (0.12in) gap between the boat and front panel, glue the collet onto the pin (you will need to put the glue on an extended rod to reach the collet).

2 From inside the box frame glue the interior arbor collet E onto the protruding arbor.

3 Turn the box frame upside down. With the small pinwheel already positioned on the crankshaft, glue the large pinwheel onto the projecting arbor so that it meshes with the small pinwheel. Some adjustment may be necessary but since at this stage the pinwheel is friction-fitted and not glued, that should not be a problem.

4 The meshing of the pins may work better in some positions than others. When you find the best arrangement, mark the relevant pins so the position is recorded.

5 When satisfied you have the best arrangement, superglue the small pinwheel to the crankshaft.

Finishing off

1 Pin and glue the top panel C on Plan 3 to the top edges of the front, back and side panels, as indicated.

2 Glue the sea panel A on Plan 4, with its supports, flush with the side panels as indicated by the dotted lines on E Plan 3. Wind the piece clockwise only.

ABOVE: *A worm's eye view shows the crankshaft, interior collet and small pinwheel enmeshed in the larger pinwheel. The cogs above, attached to the waves, rest upon their washers.*

ABOVE RIGHT: *The boat and waves are shown at their highest point. As the right-hand cogwheel is cranked anti-clockwise it turns the other cogwheel clockwise. This sets up the rolling up and down motion of the boat and waves, arranged in depth.*

RIGHT: *The boat and waves are seen at their lowest point. With the sea panel in place the fish and waves disappear behind it. Different permutations of the action can be arranged and tested to give various performances.*

ABOVE LEFT: Detail showing the fish performing behind the sea panel which has been sponged with watery blue paint on a white ground to give the effect of flashing foam.

ABOVE: Detail of the boat at its lowest point with the bow almost beneath the waves – which is where the fish are.

LEFT: The top panel extends only to two thirds to allow more light and a clearer view of the proceedings.

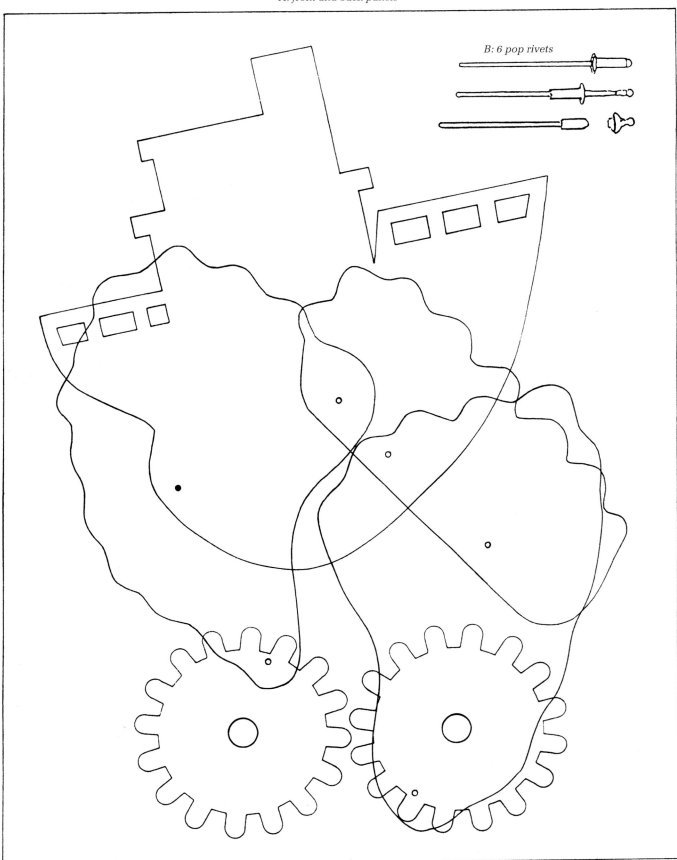

B: 6 pop rivets

×2

9

Plan 1

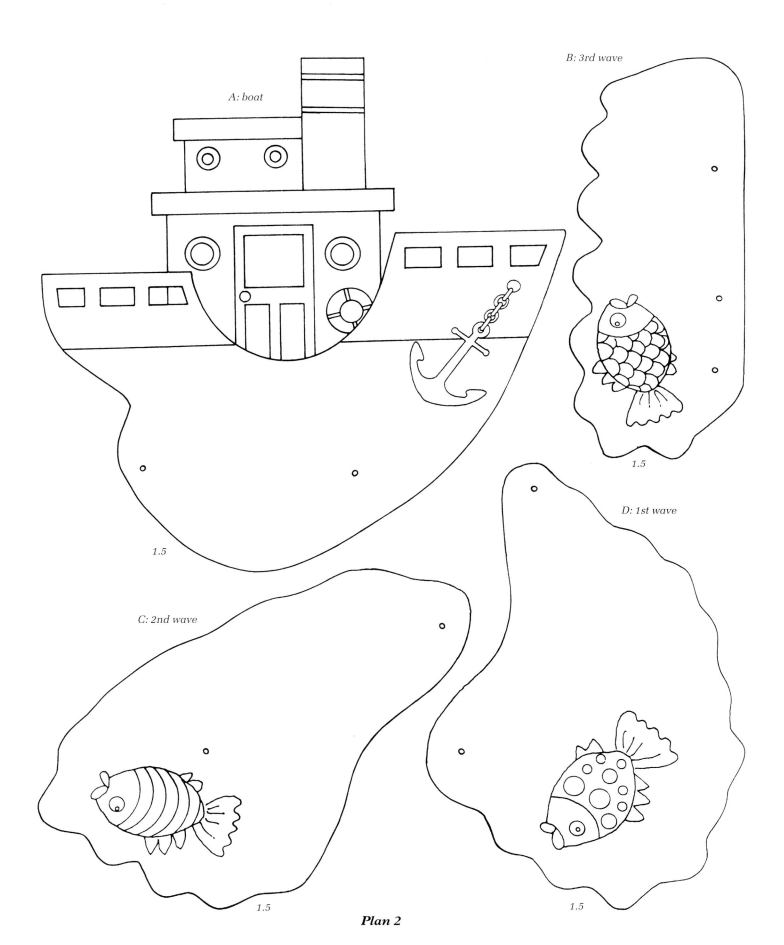

A: boat

B: 3rd wave

1.5

D: 1st wave

1.5

C: 2nd wave

1.5

1.5

Plan 2

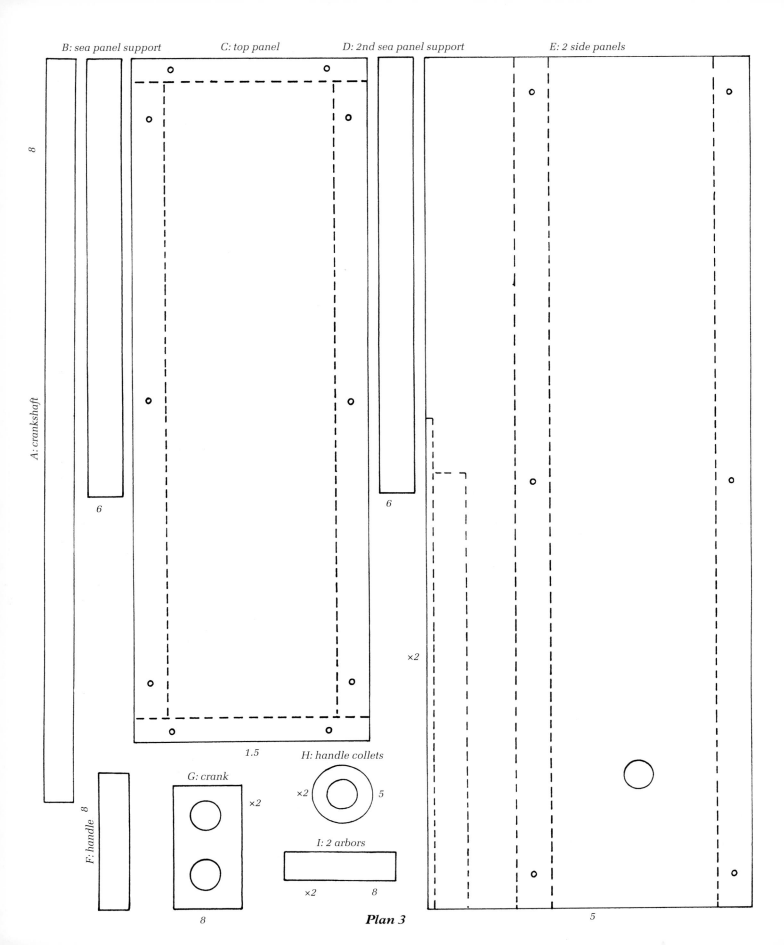

B: sea panel support *C: top panel* *D: 2nd sea panel support* *E: 2 side panels*

8

A: crankshaft

6

6

×2

1.5

H: handle collets

G: crank

F: handle *8*

×2

×2 *5*

I: 2 arbors

×2 *8*

8

5

Plan 3

A: sea panel

1.5

B/C: exterior arbor washers

D: cogwheel

E: interior arbor collet

F: interior boat collet

5

5

G: 2nd cogwheel

I: large pinwheel

5

5

5

H: small pinwheel

5

5

Plan 4

15 THE BLUEBELLES

This is a companion piece to 'A Different Drummer' (*see* Chapter 5). Like the individualistic drummer, the blonde dancer in the middle has her own ideas about self-expression. While the other troupers kick up their right legs she confidently favours her left – and vice-versa. True, she is blushing, but that is merely because she is the centre of attention.

The piece can only be turned anti-clockwise, with ten short cams engaging the back of the skirts to kick up the legs and ten long cams to move the free-swinging arms. Because of the number of cams and limb followers to be synchronized it is a fairly tricky piece to make with a lot of repetitive work. However, perseverance should be amply rewarded by the degree of humorous animation in the finished article.

MATERIALS

PLYWOOD	240 × 380 × 9mm (9.45 × 14.97 × 0.36in)	Stage, wing curtains, architrave, backdrop
STRIPWOOD	50 × 14 × 5mm (1.97 × 0.55 × 0.20in)	Crank
	525 × 4 × 4mm (20.67 × 0.16 × 0.16in)	Limbs, cams
BATTENING (PSE)	200 × 18 × 12mm (7.87 × 0.71 × 0.47in)	Five bodies
DOWEL	750 × 6mm (29.53 × 0.24in)	Camshaft, support rods, handle, necks
	50 × 16mm (1.97 × 0.63in)	Two collets
WOODEN BEADS	15mm (0.59in)	Five heads
	12mm (0.47in)	Ten breasts
PIANO WIRE	100 × 1.5mm (3.94 × 0.06in)	Five leg spindles
Five photocopies of Plan 1		

Cutting out the Bluebelles

1 You will need five photocopies of Plan 2 to spray-glue multiple parts for cutting out.
2 Cut out five bodies P on Plan 1 from battening (or plywood) but not the slots yet.
3 Cut five pairs of arms I from stripwood. Cut them in pairs (with one to spare) by temporarily bonding them together.

The Bluebelles.
158 × 280 × 95mm (6.22 × 11.03 × 3.75in).

4 Cut five pairs of legs J from stripwood. Again, cut them in pairs (with one to spare).
5 Cut five pairs of breasts by cutting in half five wooden beads 12mm (0.47in), leaving a hole in the centre of each breast. To keep the beads steady for easier cutting, insert a thin dowel through each hole.

Drilling holes in the figures and limbs

1 Drill a 6mm (0.24in) hole in each body P on Plan 1 for the neck recesses, to the depth indicated by the dotted line.

2 Drill a lateral 1.5mm (0.06in) hole through the base of the bodies, as indicated by the dotted line.

3 Drill two 1.5mm (0.06in) holes in the chests as register marks to line up with the holes in the breasts.

4 Drill a lateral (0.06in) hole through each of the shoulders, as indicated by the dotted line.

5 Drill a 6mm (0.24in) hole in each of the five heads G from 15mm (0.59in) wooden beads to the depth indicated by the dotted line.

6 From the back, drill a 6mm (0.24in) hole in each body to a depth of 7mm (0.28in). The depth is not marked on the plan.

7 Cut five necks H from dowel. Tap and glue them into the heads to the depth indicated by the dotted line.

8 Cut out the two slots for the legs from the body P.

9 With the pairs of limbs still temporarily bonded together, drill a 1.5mm (0.06in) hole in each leg J as indicated.

10 Drill a 1.5mm (0.06in) hole in each arm I.

11 Take the limbs apart for painting. Be sure to keep all the small components safely in a tin, bag or box.

Cutting out the proscenium assembly

1 Cut out the stage A on Plan 1 from plywood.

2 Cut out the two wing curtains O from plywood. If possible, cut both simultaneously by temporarily bonding two pieces of plywood together.

3 Drill a 7mm (0.28in) bearing through both wing curtains, then take them apart.

4 Cut the backdrop A on Plan 2 from plywood.

5 Drill five 6mm (0.24in) holes in the backdrop as indicated.

6 Cut out the architrave B from plywood.

Cutting the camshaft, cams, handles and support rods

1 Cut the camshaft M on Plan 1 from dowel.

2 Cut five pairs of arm cams K and five pairs of leg cams L from stripwood. However, before you do so, drill 6mm (0.24in) holes in them to prevent splitting.

3 Cut the handle C from dowel.

4 Cut the crank B from stripwood. Drill two 6mm (0.24in) holes at either end.

5 Cut the handle collet D and end stop collet E from dowel. Drill 6mm (0.24in) holes in them.

6 Cut five support rods N from dowel.

7 There are so many little pieces bent on getting lost, so curb their wanderlust with a self-sealing plastic bag.

Assembling the camshaft and its components

1 Tap and glue the handle C on Plan 1 into a hole in the crank B.

2 Friction-fit the handle collet D onto the end of the camshaft.

3 Friction-fit the camshaft M into the other hole in the crank, with the collet next to the crank.

4 The cams are friction-fitted to the camshaft in a sequence to lift the legs and move the arms alternately. Look at the illustration of the camshaft which shows how to assemble the cams. Final positioning is done when the camshaft is inserted in its bearings.

5. The illustration shows that the cams for the blonde in the middle are reversed from the flanking cams. The brunettes all kick in step with identically positioned cams, leaving our blonde friend to kick out of step.

Priming and painting the Bluebelles

1 Refer to the notes on priming and painting (*see* p.11).

2 Prime the parts to be painted with matt (vinyl) white emulsion by referring to the illustrations. (Don't paint the camshaft and cams, collets, crank handles or support rods.)

The camshaft is shown with long cams to operate the arms and short cams to work the legs. The crank handle, collet and end stop are shown below, while the wing curtains, with bearings for the camshaft, are shown above.

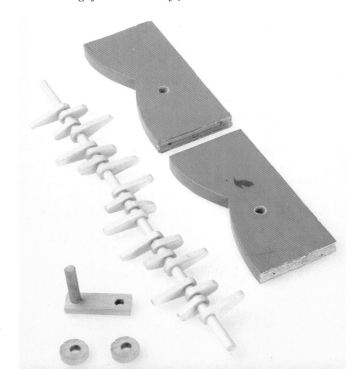

Each dancer has movable arms and legs and is supported by a rod. The skirts are followers to the short cams and the arms are followers to the long cams.

3 Paint a pink flesh coat on all the primed white areas as a first coat.
4 Paint the breasts blue, but don't obscure the bead holes as you need to register these over the two chest holes drilled in the bodies.
5 Glue the breasts to the upper bodies registering them over each chest hole. (Use a panel pin to ensure the fit.)
6 Paint stars or, ideally, stick on small metallic silver stars over the bead holes.
7 Paint blue long gloves, short skirts and shoes by referring to the illustration of a dancer.
8 Paint the heads, referring to the illustrations. The blonde in the middle needs to blush pink.

Assembling the Bluebelles

1 Friction-fit the necks (which are glued into the heads) into the bodies so that the brunettes all look towards the blonde in the middle, while she looks dead ahead.
2 Using household pins, clip them to length to fit through the small arm/shoulder holes and into the lateral holes in the upper bodies. Superglue the arms in position, not too tightly, ensuring they can move freely.
3 Cut five leg spindles Q on Plan 1 from 1.5mm (0.06in) piano wire. Insert them, cut to length, through the bodies and legs so that the legs swing easily within the slots. Superglue the spindles at their outer ends and touch up with blue paint to cover the holes.

4 Glue the support rods N into the holes in the back of the bodies. (These rods, when fitted into the backdrop, will protrude about 12mm (0.47in) to facilitate positioning the dancers.)

Priming and painting the proscenium and stage

1 Prime the stage A on Plan 1 with matt (vinyl) white emulsion, leaving bare wood as indicated by the dotted lines to facilitate gluing.
2 Prime the wing curtains O white on all sides except their base edges.
3 Prime the backdrop A on Plan 2 white, except the side edges as indicated by the dotted lines.
4 Prime the architrave B white all over.
5 Paint the stage beige, the wing curtains and architrave deep pink and the backdrop, mauve.
6 Make a stencil of the arrow on the (handle end) wing curtain. Spray-glue a photocopy of the arrow onto a sheet of paper and cut out the arrow.
7 Lightly spray-glue the arrow stencil on the back and, when dry, position it as indicated above the camshaft bearing. Dab blue paint into it with a stencil brush.
8 Transfer the design to the architrave and paint it white.

A rear view of the figure shows the embedded support rod and the breast register holes either side. The free-swinging limbs are struck by the cams to create kicking legs and swinging arms.

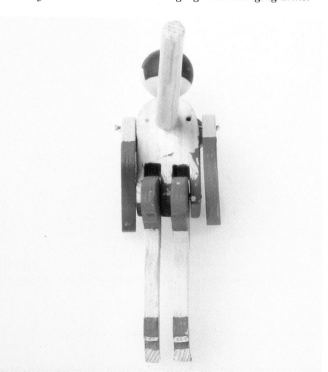

The architrave design can either be transferred and painted or cut out and stencilled. A circles template is required for the former method and a hole punch is required for the latter.

Assembling the proscenium and stage

1   Pin the stage A on Plan 1, as indicated, to the base edge of the backdrop B on Plan 2 (with the holes nearest the top) as indicated by the dotted lines. (No gluing yet.)
2   Pin the stage A, as indicated, to the base edges of the wing curtains O as indicated by the dotted lines.
3   Pin the back drop A on Plan 2, as indicated by the two holes at either end, to the back edges of the wing curtains as indicated by the dotted lines. Leave the pins projecting out a fraction so you that you will be able to withdraw them later.
4   Drill vertical 1.5mm (0.06in) pilot holes for 30mm (1.18in) panel pins in the outer ends of the architrave B as indicated by the dotted lines.
5   Pin the architrave through the pilot holes either end into the top edge of the backdrop A.

Inserting the camshaft and gluing the proscenium

1   Remove the friction-fitted crank handle and collet from the end of the camshaft.
2   The wing curtains, architrave and backdrop are only pinned in position and can be removed to install the camshaft. Withdraw the two pins at the back of the backdrop (which you left proud) until they are clear of the wing curtains.
3   Remove the architrave from the wing curtains and then withdraw the wing curtain from the stage.

4   Insert the end of the camshaft (with its friction-fitted cams) into the wing curtain bearing (without the arrow) and glue the base and back edge of the curtain pressing it back onto the two pins.
5   Insert the other end of the camshaft into the inside bearing of the wing curtain (with the arrow). Glue the base and back edge of the curtain pressing down on the two pins.
6   Now, tap in the two pins at the top of the backdrop so that the wing curtains are now both glued to the stage and backdrop.
7   Replace the crank handle and collet, gluing them to the end of the crankshaft.
8   Glue the collet end stop E on Plan 1 to the other end of the shaft, leaving plenty of space between it and the curtain. About 5mm (0.20in) is left protruding (this is for aesthetic, not mechanical, reasons).

Inserting the dancers on their support rods

1   Insert the support rods of the dancers into the holes

The camshaft is shown resting within its bearings in the two wing curtains which are fixed to the stage. An anti-clockwise arrow shows the only way to turn the handle.

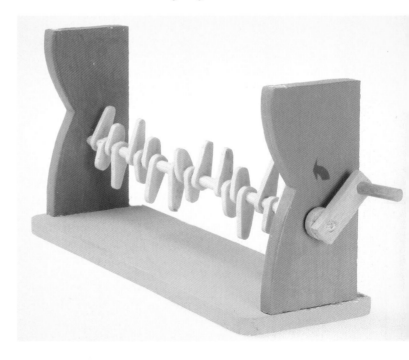

in the backdrop, leaving about 12mm (0.47in) protruding. (As mentioned earlier, this is to facilitate positioning the dancers.)

2 It will be seen that the cams are approximately in the correct positions to engage the followers (or limbs). Fine tuning is now required. Each cam must move an arm or a leg without jamming. (Long cams for arms, short for legs.)

3 Jamming occurs when the shoes get caught on the stage. Filing off the excess may help; alternatively, try moving the offending figure backwards or forwards on the support rod.

4 You can move the cams laterally to engage the followers, but do not twist them out of their parallel positions. The brunettes must all kick in step with only the blonde in the middle doing her own thing.

5 When satisfied that all members of the troupe are performing as desired, superglue the cams all the way round. Be careful not to get glue on the dancers.

6 Remember: the piece only turns anti-clockwise.

The dancers are positioned on their rods, supported by the backdrop, with the long cams moving their arms and the short cams operating their kicking legs.

If the piece jams in operation it is possibly because the shoes get caught on the stage. The soles may need filing to eliminate this. The support rods are friction-fitted, which allows backward and forward adjustment.

The architrave is shown fixed to either end of the wing curtains. While the brunettes kick their right legs the star kicks her left.

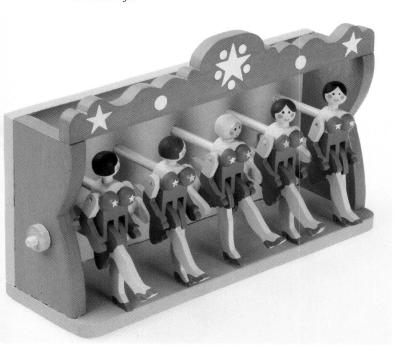

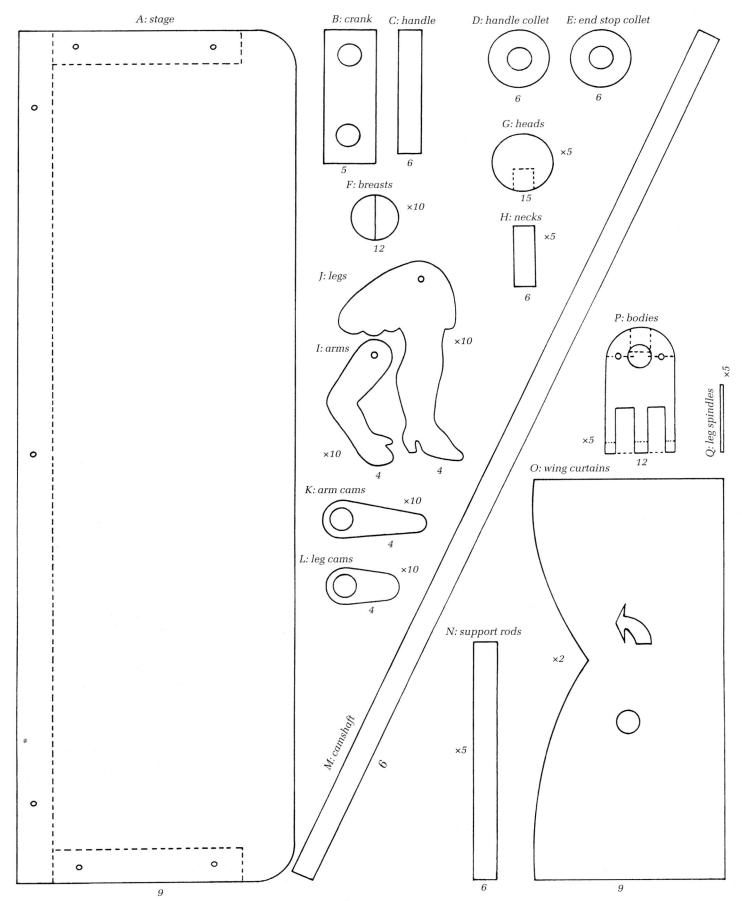

Plan 1

A: backdrop

B: architrave

9

9

Plan 2

16 TWO-HEADED STRONGMAN

As an homage to the Belgian surrealist painter René Magritte (1898–1967), this piece reflects his painting of the weight lifter whose dumb-bell is replaced by a head. At the turn of a wrist (and this is where our athlete diverges from Magritte's) two heads rotate laterally, changing places: a moustachioed macho face and a sympathetic poetic face, shedding a tear.

When continuously wound, the heads alternate, pausing at the neck and pausing again as they point towards one. East to West shows the macho head; North to South shows the dumb-bell at right angles to the body. East to West now shows the poetic head. This is achieved by the Geneva wheel mechanism which is really a ratchet device, like a film projector's which advances each frame one at a time.

Two pinwheels have been introduced to turn the mechanism from the side. Any toy involving handmade pinwheels recommends itself to the more experienced toymakers and this one is no exception. The Geneva wheel mechanism is a joy to behold and to see it working compounds the joy.

MATERIALS

PLYWOOD	400 × 220 × 9mm (15.75 × 8.66 × 0.36in)	Strongman, box panels, two pinwheel
	180 × 80 × 6mm (7.09 × 3.15 × 0.24in)	Cross, shield, crank wheel
AEROPLY	140 × 120 × 1.5mm (5.5 × 4.72 × 0.06in)	Front panel
DOWEL	45 × 16mm (1.77 × 0.63in)	Two collets
	410 × 6mm (16.15 × 0.24in)	Arbor, handle, crankshaft, vertical rod
	20 × 3mm (0.79 × 0.12in)	Crank pin
STRIPWOOD	90 × 12 × 12mm (3.54 × 0.47 × 0.47in)	Support post
	45 × 15 × 5mm (1.77 × 0.59 × 0.20in)	Crank
METAL WASHER	1 × 20mm (0.04 × 0.79in)	
MASKING TAPE	13mm (0.51in) wide	
SCREWS	30mm (1.18in) No.8, countersunk	
Stencil brush		

Cutting out the Strongman

1 Cut out the block (along the dotted line) with a photocopy of Plan 1 spray-glued onto plywood.

Two-Headed Strongman.
254 × 184 × 67mm (10 × 7.25 × 2.64in).

2 Before cutting out the Strongman, drill a central 7mm (0.28in) hole vertically through the forearm as indicated by the dotted lines.

3 Turn over the block and drill two vertical 4mm (0.16in) holes for No. 8 screws in each thigh, as indicated by the dotted lines.

4　Cut out the Strongman from the block, separating the head from the neck and cutting away the waste between the forearm and head.

5　When the figure is completely cut out, cut the dumb-bell free at the dotted line beneath the wrist.

Cutting out the box

1　Cut out the base A on Plan 2 from plywood. Drill a 7mm (0.28in) hole in it as indicated.

2　Cut out the shelf I from plywood. Drill two 7mm (0.28in) holes in it as indicated.

3　Cut out the side panels A and B on Plan 3 from ply-wood. If possible, cut them simultaneously by tem-porarily bonding two pieces of plywood together (note that panel B should be placed over A when temporarily bonding).

4　Drill six 1mm (0.04in) pilot holes for panel pins, top and bottom, as indicated.

5　Separate the panels (if temporarily bonded) and cut out the slot from side panel A.

6　Drill a 7mm (0.28in) bearing in side panel B.

7　Cut out the top panel E from plywood. Drill two 4mm (0.16in) pilot holes for No.8 screws within the two dotted line rectangles.

8　Drill a 7mm (0.28in) hole for the vertical rod as indi-cated. Drill four pilot holes for panel pins in the four corners, as indicated.

9　Cut out the front panel G on Plan 2 from Aeroply.

Assembling the box

1　Refer to the notes on making boxes (see pp12–13).

2　Pin and glue the slotted side panel A on Plan 3 to the base A on Plan 2, nearest the hole.

3　Pin and glue the bearing side panel B on Plan 3 to the other end of the base A on Plan 2.

4　Pin and glue the shelf I between the two side panels within the dotted lines.

5　Pin, but do not glue, the top panel E on Plan 3 to the top edges of the side panels as indicated: the feet at the handle end of the panel.

6　Pin, but do not glue, the front panel G on Plan 2 to the front edges of the other panels.

Making the Geneva wheel mechanism

1　Cut out the cross B on Plan 2, the shield F and the crank wheel H from 6mm (0.24in) plywood.

2　Drill central 6mm (0.24in) holes in the cross, the shield and crank wheel. Drill a 3mm (0.12in) hole near the rim of the crank wheel, as shown.

3　Glue the shield F to the crank wheel H as indicated by the dotted line.

4　Cut the crank pin D and arbor E from dowels.

5　Tap and glue the crank pin into the small hole near the rim of the crank wheel, flush with its base.

6　Turn the crank wheel and shield over and tap and glue the arbor through the bonded components, flush with the surface of the shield.

7　Keep the components safely, together with the cross which will complete the mechanism.

Making the pinwheel

1　Cut out the pinwheels K and L on Plan 3. Drill twelve 1.5mm (0.06in) holes in each pinwheel.

2　Drill central 6mm (0.24in) holes in them. It is impor-tant that these holes are drilled accurately and the use of a pillar drill, or drill stand attachment to a power drill, is strongly recommended.

3　Tap 30mm (1.18in)-long panel pins into all the holes but one, on both wheels. The gaps allow you to fit the nose of your snips into each circle of pins.

The Geneva wheel components show the cross and shield, the crank wheel and pin.

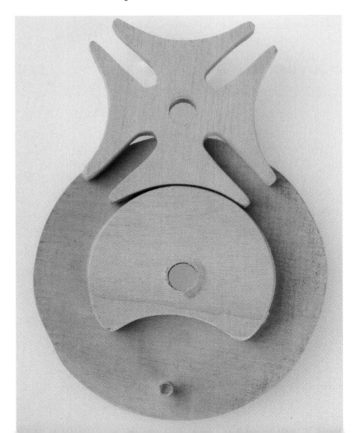

4 Cut the panel pins 14mm (0.55in) above the surface of each pinwheel.

5 Insert the two remaining pins and snip them to the same length as the other pins.

6 Wrap a length of 13mm (0.51in) masking tape around each circle of pins. File the tops of the pins with the aid of a belt sander or circular sander, so that the pins are level with the tape.

7 Remove the tape and you have two identical pinwheels with pins at a uniform height.

Cutting the handle and other components

1 Cut the handle G on Plan 3 from dowel.

2 Cut the crank H from stripwood. Drill 6mm (0.24in) holes in both ends.

3 Cut the exterior and interior collets I and J from dowel. Drill 6mm (0.24in) holes in them.

4 Cut the crankshaft F from dowel.

5 Cut the vertical rod D from dowel.

6 Cut the support post C from stripwood. Drill a 7mm (0.28in) hole in it as indicated.

7 Tap and glue the handle into the crank.

8 Tap and glue the crankshaft into the other hole in the crank.

9 Place the exterior collet I onto the crankshaft and glue it to the crank.

10 Put the interior collet J onto the crankshaft for safe-keeping until later.

Priming and painting

1 See the notes on priming and painting (*see* p.11).

2 Prime both sides of the Strongman and dumb-bell with matt (vinyl) white emulsion.

3. Prime the outside parts of the box with matt (vinyl) white emulsion.

4. Prime the crank handle assembly with matt (vinyl) white emulsion.

5 Sand down all the primed surfaces and transfer the design (*see* the notes) of the Strongman to the primed surface.

6 Follow the illustrations for colour reference. Use an off-white or cream paint for the box and tee-shirt. A circles template (obtainable from art shops) will help to draw the medals and studs. They should be painted silver, together with the ring on the front panel.

7 Create a stencil by spray-gluing a photocopy of the front panel G on Plan 2 onto paper and then cutting

out the design within the circle. Spray-glue the back of the stencil and position it lightly over the front panel.

8 Replace the star in the centre of the stencil and pin prick the central dot. With ruling pen and compass, draw and paint the silver ring.

9 Using a stencil brush, dab blue paint into the stars and red paint into the hearts, as shown in the illustrations.

10 Now, do the same to colour the blue stars on the side panels.

11 Paint the handle blue and the crank and collet, red.

The decoration is achieved by cutting a stencil for the hearts and stars and using a ruling pen and compass for the silver ring.

Inserting part of the Geneva mechanism and pin wheels

1 Remove the top panel which is only pinned, not glued, to the side panels.

2 Insert the arbor of the crank wheel assembly E/F/H on Plan 2 through the metal washer C into the hole in the shelf, nearest the crank.

3 Friction-fit (to allow for adjustment) a pinwheel from under the shelf onto the protruding arbor, but don't fit the wheel too tightly.

4 Glue the support post C on Plan 3, top and bottom, to the base indicated by the dotted rule square and to the underside of the shelf. Ensure that it is perpendicular and that the bearing lines up with the bearing in the side panel.

5 Remove the interior collet from the camshaft. Insert the camshaft into the side panel bearing and replace the collet onto the camshaft, inside the box.

6 Friction-fit the other pinwheel onto the crankshaft and move the interior collet and pinwheel along the shaft towards the handle. At the same time, fit the end of the crankshaft into the bearing in the support post.

7 Move the pinwheel back along the camshaft until it engages the other pinwheel. Pinwheels, because they are handmade, don't always enmesh easily. A degree of experimentation will be required to find the best combination of pins to avoid jams.

8 When the best positions for the wheels are found, mark the opposing pins (with a black spirit marker) so you can easily find them again. Only when certain that you have the best permutation should you superglue the pinwheel to the crankshaft.

9 The other (friction-fitted) pinwheel can be glued where the end of the arbor is visible.

10 Glue the interior collet about 1mm (0.04in) away from the bearing in the side panel to allow a little play on the crankshaft. The mechanism is now sealed.

Inserting the rest of the Geneva mechanism

1 Screw two 30mm (1.18in) long countersunk No. 8 screws into the pilot holes in the underside of the top panel E on Plan 3 as indicated.

2 Screw into the figure's thighs (facing front) as indicated by the dotted lines on Plan 1.

3 Insert the vertical rod D on Plan 3 through the Strongman's forearm and the hole in the top panel.

A detail shows a part of the Geneva mechanism, without the cross. Part of the pin wheel attached to the central arbor can be seen with the bearing in the support post on the left.

4 Friction-fit the cross B on Plan 2 onto the vertical rod, under the top panel and above the shelf, sandwiched between them with plenty of space. The rod rests in the hole in the base, just clear of the ground.

5 Engage the crank pin, on the outer edge of the crank wheel, with one of the slots in the cross. Turn the crank handle and test the completed Geneva wheel mechanism. The cross should move freely over the wheel, pausing at every rotation, as the crank pin engages the slots.

6 When satisfied that the mechanism is working efficiently, the head rotating with pauses at the neck and again head-on, the cross can be glued in position on the rod.

7 The removable top can now be glued and pinned in position over the other panels.

8 Pin and glue the front panel to the edges of the other panels.

9. The piece can rotate clockwise or anti-clockwise and has an open-to-view mechanism, without a back panel.

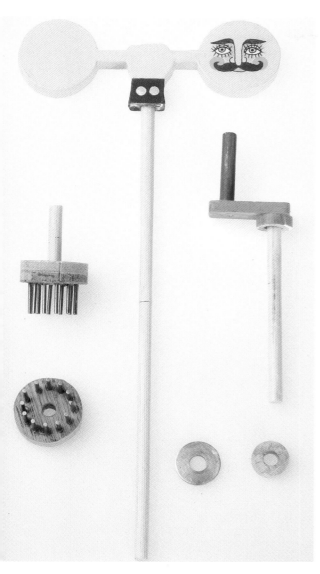

The torso is screwed to the top panel which has a vertical channel drilled through the forearm to receive the vertical rod.

The layout of components shows the dumb-bell and hand supported by the vertical rod. The pinwheels are shown on the left while the crankshaft and handle, a washer and interior collet are on the right.

The underside of the top panel shows the cross element of the Geneva wheel mechanism positioned on the vertical rod.

BELOW LEFT: A rear view shows the 'poetic' head and the interior mechanism. The crank drives the pinwheels which turn the Geneva wheel. The crank pin is seen on the left, the cross on the right.

BELOW: A front view shows the macho head and the interior mechanism. The crankshaft rests on the bearing in the support post on the left. The vertical rod is held by the hole in the base.

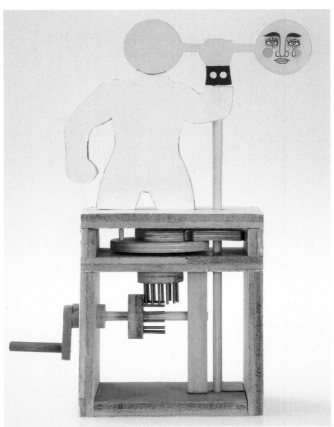

The dumb-bell is shown head on, between one of the pauses for the changing heads, provided by the Geneva wheel mechanism.

Strongman

Plan 1

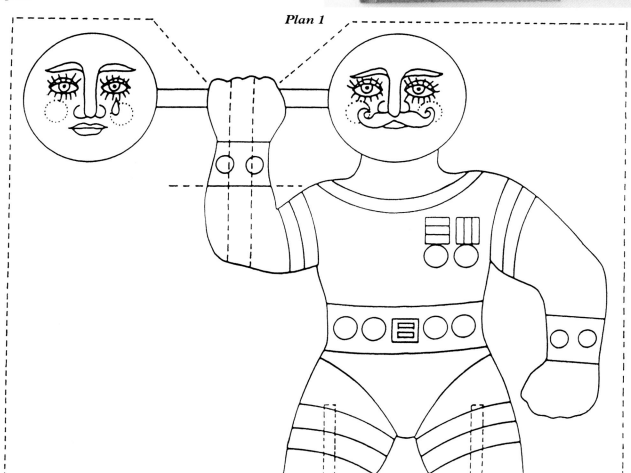

9

A: base

B: cross

C: metal washer

1

F: shield

6

6

D: crank pin

3

E: arbor

6

H: crank wheel

6

9

G: front panel

I: shelf

9

1.5

Plan 2

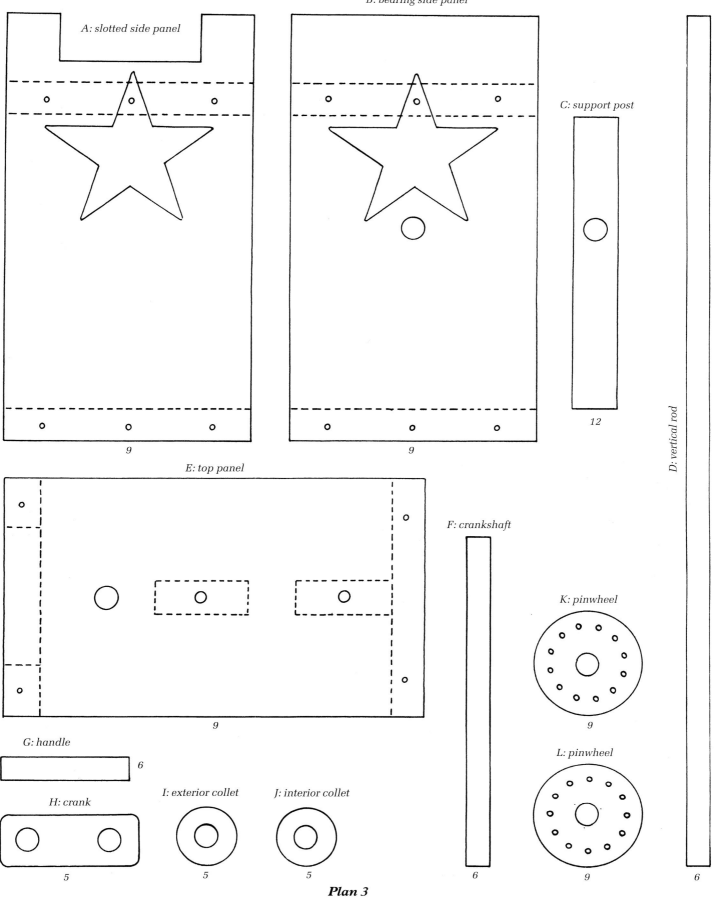

A: slotted side panel

B: bearing side panel

C: support post

D: vertical rod

E: top panel

F: crankshaft

G: handle

H: crank

I: exterior collet

J: interior collet

K: pinwheel

L: pinwheel

9

9

12

9

6

6

5

5

5

6

9

9

Plan 3

17 JUNGLE BOX

A deserted jungle fills up with animals as strings are pulled and locked into position. One by one they appear: a monkey, a tiger, a lion, a giraffe, a snake, a toucan, a tortoise, an elephant, a rhinoceros, a leopard and an alligator. Each animal panel has a string attached to the base which, when pulled over a bar, lifts the animal through the jungle floor. When the string is released, gravity lends a hand.

It takes about five seconds to clear the jungle by flicking the beads off their rests. Invite a child to find a favourite animal. After a while it will become apparent which string works which animal and a 'Kim' game evolves as the child remembers the identity and position of each animal. The play value is considerable.

The reader has the choice of whether to paint the animals or use colour copies of the designs to spray-glue onto plywood and cut out. The jungle is painted light green and dry-sponged with a dark green to give a leafy effect. It is a piece for the more experienced maker.

MATERIALS

PLYWOOD	255 × 186 × 9mm (10.04 × 7.32 × 0.36in)	Jungle floor
	735 × 399 × 5mm (28.94 × 15.71 × 0.20in)	Five box panels
	356 × 254 × 5mm (14.02 × 10 × 0.20in)	Foliage
	375 × 100 × 3mm (14.77 × 3.49 × 0.12in)	Channel slots
AEROPLY	450 × 330 × 1.5mm (17.72 × 12.99 × 0.06in)	Animal panels
	375 × 155 × 1.5mm (14.77 × 6.1 × 0.06in)	Panel supports
STRIPWOOD	675 × 6 × 6mm (26.57 × 0.24 × 0.24in)	Eleven baffle supports, eleven bead rests, eight foliage supports
	275 × 15 × 8mm (10.83 × 0.59 × 0.32in)	Fifteen bar supports
BATTENING (PSE)	290 × 26 × 12mm (11.41 × 1.02 × 0.59in)	Support blocks
PIANO WIRE: TWO LENGTHS	914mm and 2.5mm (36in and 0.10in)	
PLASTIC TUBING	914 × 2.5mm (36 × 0.10in)	
POLYSTYRENE DAMP PROOF COVERING	152 × 152 × 1mm (6 × 6 × 0.04in)	
THIN STRING	8,382mm (330in)	

Jungle Box.
290 × 245 × 185mm (11.41 × 9.44 × 7.29in).

Cutting out the animal panels

1 You have the choice of whether to paint the animals yourself from the colour illustrations or to make

colour photocopies to spray-glue and cut out from plywood.

2 If the latter method is chosen, substitute colour copies of the animals on the plans by cutting along the dotted lines and exchanging black and white for colour designs.

3 Cut out the snake panel B on Plan 3 from Aeroply.

4 Cut out the monkey A, the tortoise B, the rhino C and the leopard G panels on Plan 4 from Aeroply.

5 Cut out the giraffe A, the alligator B and the lion F panels on Plan 5 from Aeroply.

6 Cut out the tiger A, the elephant B and the toucan F panels on Plan 6 from Aeroply.

7 Drill central 1.5mm (0.06in) holes at the bottom of each of the eleven panels as indicated.

8 Cut eleven lengths of 762mm (30in) thin string. Thread them through the holes in the panels, tying double knots at the back of each panel.

9 Cut eleven baffle supports M on Plan 7 from stripwood.

10 Using a Pritt-stick or similar polystyrene-compatible adhesive, glue the supports to polystyrene damp-proof wall covering. Use a sharp craft knife or scalpel to cut away the waste. You could use folded felt strips to baffle the sound, if you prefer.

11 Glue the baffle supports to the back of each animal panel as indicated, facing upwards. (These will act as stops to prevent the panels coming up too far.)

Cutting out the sliding panel supports

1 Cut out thirty (yes, thirty!) panel supports E on Plan 7 from Aeroply.

2 Cut out fifteen channel slots D from plywood.

3 Glue the channel slots to the centre of each panel support as indicated by the dotted lines.

4 Cut sixteen triangular support blocks from battening (PSE) by cutting along the diagonal on eight blocks N. (Note that only fifteen blocks are needed, so there will be one spare.)

5 Glue the fifteen triangular blocks to the bases of the panel supports as indicated by the dotted line on E.

6 Cut fifteen bar supports J from stripwood. Drill 3mm (0.12in) central holes, laterally, as shown by the dotted lines. You may prefer to drill holes in one length of stripwood 270mm (10.63in) and then cut the lengths.

7 Glue the bar supports to the top of each panel support as indicated by the dotted rectangle on E.

8 There are many little pieces that are so easy to lose. Confine them to a self-sealing plastic bag.

Cutting out the box panels

1 Cut out the two side panels A on Plan 8 from plywood. Cut both simultaneously by temporarily bonding two pieces together. Drill a 3.5mm (0.14in) hole through them as indicated.

2 Cut out the two side supports B from battening (PSE). Drill four 2.5mm (0.10in) holes in them as indicated.

3 Spray-glue a photocopy of the elevated base on Plan 9 onto plywood.

4 Temporarily bond this to plywood for the thicker jungle floor on Plan 10 and cut out the two panels together, as they are the same size.

5 Drill twenty-two 3mm (0.12in) holes in the elevated base as indicated and through the (thicker) jungle floor. Separate the panels.

6 Drill eleven 9mm (0.36in) holes (for the strings) in the elevated base which you have separated from the jungle floor.

7 Cut eleven baffle strips of polystyrene wall covering to the sizes indicated on Plan 9. Use Pritt-stick, or a

Eleven sliding panels fit into twenty-two panel supports like this to provide levitation and descent for the jungle animals. Each panel has, for this purpose, a hole for a string to be knotted at the base.

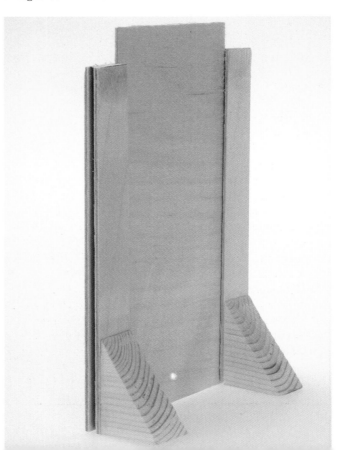

similar compatible adhesive, and glue them, as indicated, between the small holes. (If you prefer, you can use folded felt as a baffle.)

8 Spray-glue the back of the jungle floor photocopy of Plan 10. Place it accurately over the thicker panel you have just cut, ensuring that the drilled holes line up with the photocopy. If you are cutting out colour copies of the animals make the slots a little wider.

9 Either peel off the photocopy of Plan 10 or make another, because you will need the dotted rectangles to position the foliage.

10 Cut out the front and back panels on Plan 11 from plywood, temporarily bonding them together. Separate the panels.

11 Drill eleven 2.5mm (0.10in) holes along the bottom of the front panel as indicated.

12 Cut eleven 10mm (0.4in) lengths of plastic tubing 2.5mm (0.10in) thick. Tap and super-glue these into the holes in the front panel. Snip off the waste and sand them flush with the front panel. These plastic sleeves will ease friction on the strings.

Assembling the sliding animal panels

1 Glue and pin the elevated base on Plan 9 to the top of each side support panel B on Plan 8.

2 Cut four side support bars A on Plan 7 from piano wire. Insert them so they friction-fit flush with the sides of the two side supports B on Plan 8.

3 Cut four panel support bars B on Plan 7 from piano wire.

4 Cut four panel support rods C from stripwood.

5 Each of the fifteen slotted panel supports (which you assembled earlier) should be glued, with a slow drying adhesive, between the holes in the elevated base on Plan 9 as indicated by the dotted lines. The slots line up with the holes.

6 Place the animal panels (with their strings attached) into each slotted support. Refer to the illustrations or Plan 10 to see where they go.

7 Insert the four panel support bars B on Plan 7 through the (loose fitting) bar supports. Glue the ends.

8 Place the strings over the bars and feed them through the large central holes in the elevated base.

9 Glue the four panel support rods C to the panel supports and the tops of the triangular support blocks N.

10 Test the sliding panels by placing the strings under the bars (as in the illustration) on the underside of the elevated base. Some adjustments can be made at this

stage, but you will need the jungle floor in position before you can test the slots.

Assembling the jungle box

1 Refer to the notes on making boxes (*see* pp12–13).

2 Pin, but don't glue, the front and back panels on Plan 11 to the side supports B on Plan 8 which support the elevated base.

3 Gently place the jungle floor over the animals so that they are within their slots, being careful not to scuff them. Make adjustments if necessary.

4 Pin, but don't glue, the front and back panels to the front and back edges of the jungle floor.

5 Pin, but don't glue, the two side panels A to the side edges of the jungle floor. Screw a small screw through each side panel and into the side supports B as indicated. Be careful not to fasten the screw too tightly.

Cutting the foliage

1 Cut out foliage A, C and D on Plan 3 from plywood.

2 Cut out foliage D, E and F on Plan 4 from plywood.

3 Cut out foliage C, D and E on Plan 5 from plywood.

4 Cut out foliage E, C and D on Plan 6 from plywood.

5 Cut out foliage F, H and O on Plan 7 from plywood.

6 Cut out eight foliage supports G.

7 Cut out eleven bead rests L from stripwood. Drill two 1.5mm (0.06in) holes in them as indicated. The best way to do this is to mark off the lengths on the stripwood, drill the holes and then cut to length.

Painting the box and foliage

1 See the notes on priming and painting. Mark all the pieces of foliage on their bottom edges with numbers corresponding to those on Plan 10, denoted by the dotted lines, to keep track of them.

2 Score the bottom edges with a craft knife to key them for gluing.

3 Dismantle the box (using a putty knife or spatula) leaving only the elevated base and components.

4 Prime the outside of the box panels with matt (vinyl) white emulsion. Prime the foliage both sides, likewise, leaving the bottom edges unprimed and unpainted. Acrylic paints are recommended.

5 Paint the primed parts light green (sparingly in the slots), adding a second coat when dry.

6 Use a 50mm (2in) dry sponge block to dab dark green paint over the light green on everything except the jungle floor and edges. Touch up with a fine brush.

The foliage effect is achieved by dabbing dark green paint over light green, with a dry sponge.

A rear three-quarter view shows the foliage supports for the outer trees and shrubs.

Assembling the jungle foliage

1. Assemble the box as before, but now that everything is tested and working you can add glue to the operation.
2. Glue the foliage to the jungle floor and top edges of the panel, referring to the numbers marked on their bases and the relative positions as shown on Plan 10 by the dotted rectangles. All pieces face outwards except the giraffe's tree, No. 3.
3. Glue the eight foliage supports G on Plan 7 to the outer shrubs and trees. The smaller inside foliage is self-supporting.
4. Cut twenty-two bead rest panel pins I to length as shown. Tap and glue them into the bead rests L and file off their ends so they do not impair the strings.

Assembling the strings, beads and bead rests

1. Look at the illustration of the inside of the box showing the bars and strings. Thread the strings under the bars (as before) and through the plastic tubing embedded in the front panel.
2. Insert the strings into the beads and superglue them in position, at the bottom of the front panel, with their strings taut and animals out of sight. Their tops are resting, unseen, in the slots.
3. Referring to the front panel on Plan 11, pull the beads up until the baffles on the back of the animal panels can come up no further.
4. With the beads held tautly in their rests, superglue the rests to the front panel at right angles to the base, as shown on Plan 11.
5. Cut off the surplus strings.
6. Release the beads from their rests and the animals will fall beneath the jungle floor. They can be retrieved, in any order, at the pull of a string.
7. This is a difficult piece to make and it is essential that, before assembling the jungle floor, all the animals can move freely within their slots. It is irritating to find parts sticking once they have been installed!

The underside of the Jungle Box shows the animals' strings passing under the bars, through the holes in the front panel and held by wooden beads on rests made from panel pins.

BELOW: An interior side view shows the panels lifted to their highest point revealing the animals. Baffles at the top, made from polystyrene to deaden the sound, check the level of ascent.

BELOW RIGHT: The same view shows the panel lowered, by gravity, once the beads are removed from their rests. The bar supports at the top contain long bars for each row of animals. The panel support rods, likewise, run the full length of the box, for extra stability.

A: snake

When the beads are on their rests the jungle is full of animals.

B: toucan

C: monkey

D: tortoise

When the beads are off their rests, the jungle is empty.

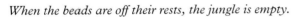

E: lion   **Plan 1**

A: giraffe

B: alligator

C: leopard

D: rhinoceros

F: tiger

Plan 2

E: elephant

A: foliage 5

5

5

B: snake panel

1.5

C: foliage 3 (giraffe's tree)

3

5

D: foliage 4

4

5

Plan 3

A: monkey panel

B: tortoise panel

C: rhinoceros panel

1.5

1.5

1.5

D: foliage 13

13

5

E: foliage 15

15

5

F: foliage 8

8

5

G: leopard panel

1.5

Plan 4

A: giraffe panel

B: alligator panel

1.5

1.5

C: foliage 10

10

5

D: foliage 14

5

14

E: foliage 6

6

5

F: lion panel

1.5

Plan 5

A: tiger panel

B: elephant panel

1.5

1.5

C: foliage 12

12

5

D: foliage 11

11

5

5

E: foliage 9

9

F: toucan panel

1.5

Plan 6

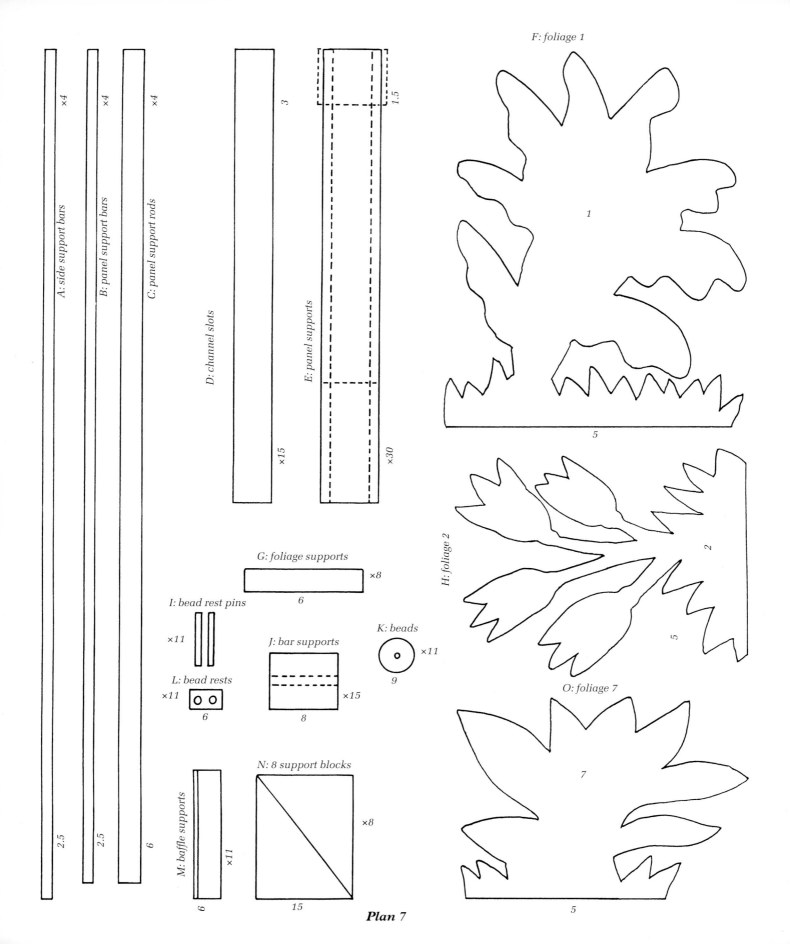

F: foliage 1

1

5

A: side support bars ×4

B: panel support bars ×4

C: panel support rods ×4

D: channel slots

E: panel supports

3

1.5

×15

×30

2.5

2.5

6

H: foliage 2

2

5

G: foliage supports ×8

6

I: bead rest pins ×11

J: bar supports

K: beads ×11

9

L: bead rests ×11

6

×15

8

O: foliage 7

7

5

M: baffle supports ×11

N: 8 support blocks ×8

6

15

Plan 7

A: side panels

5

×2

B: side supports

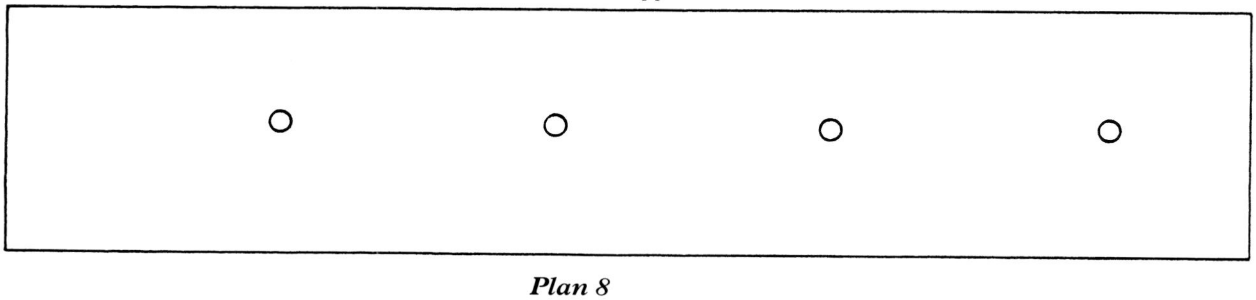

12

×2

Plan 8

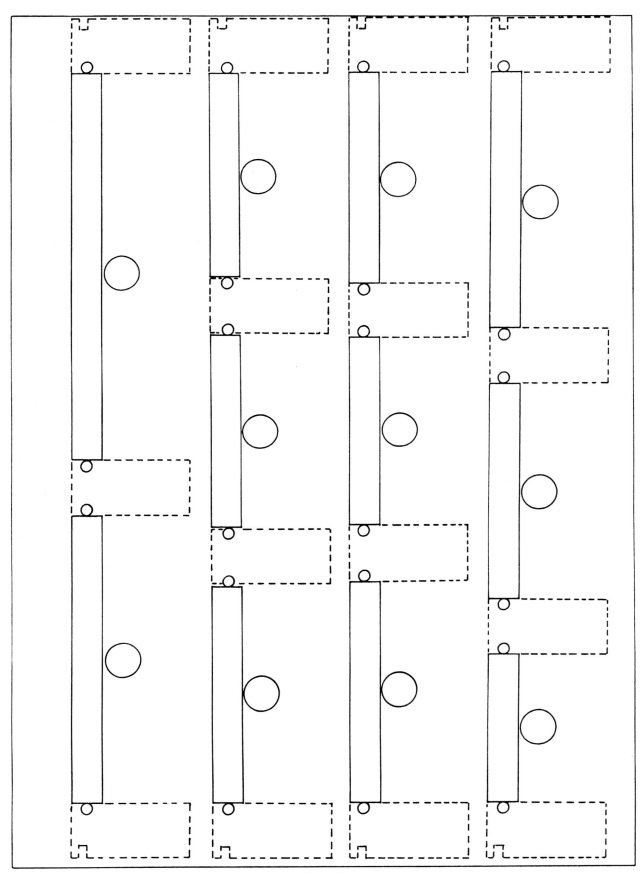

Plan 9

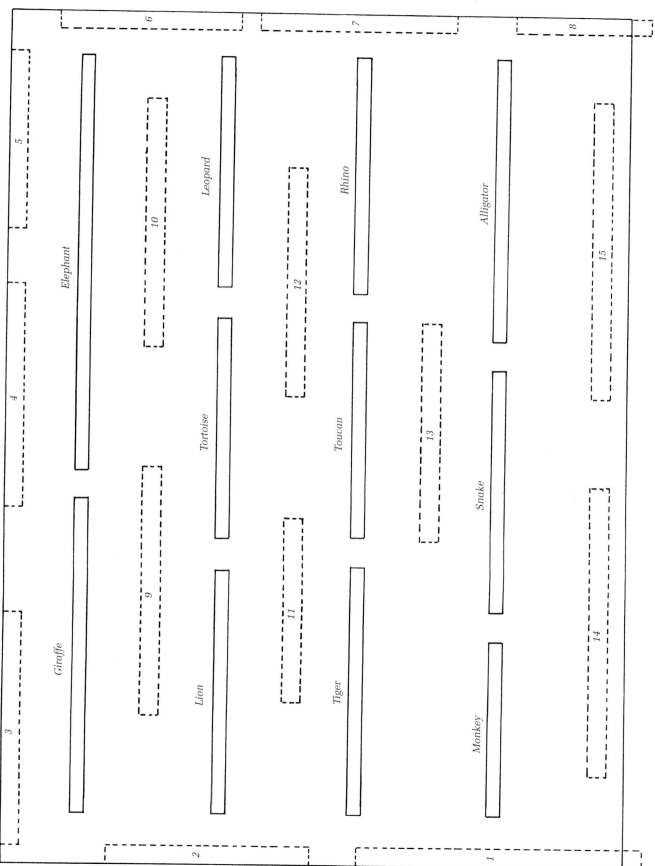

Plan 10

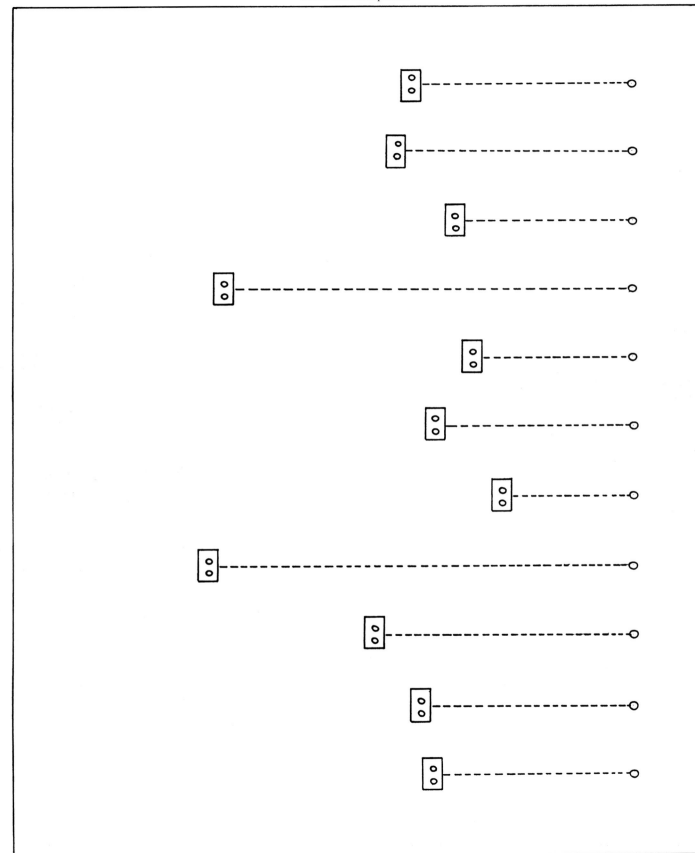

Plan 11

BIBLIOGRAPHY

Some of the following titles may be out of print but may be found in libraries and second-hand bookshops.

Bacon, M., *No Strings Attached* (Virgin, 1997; ISBN 1 85227669x)
   An account of Jim Henson's Creature Shop and details of the application of Animatronics in films.

Bailly, C. with Bailly, S., *Automata – The Golden Age 1848–1914* (Sotheby's Publications, 1987; Philip Wilson Publishers Ltd; ISBN 0 85667 345 5)

Bartholemew, C., *Mechanical Toys* (Hamlyn, 1979; ISBN 0 600 363 317)

Bishop, R. and Coblenz, P., *A Gallery of American Weathervanes and Whirligigs* (E P Dutton, New York, 1981; ISBN 0 525 93151 1)

Brown, H.T., *507 Mechanical Movements* (first published 1868; US edition published by Lindsay, 1984; ISBN 991791 425 2)

Carrea, R., *Androids – The Jaquet-Droz Automatons* (Scriptar SA, Lausanne, 1979; ISBN 2 88012 0187)

Chapuis, A. and Droz, E., *Automata: A historical and technological study* (originally published by Editions du Griffon, Neuchatel, Switzerland, 1958; translated into English by Alec Reid, and published by Central Book Co. Inc., New York; ISBN unknown)

Cielisk, J. and M., *Lehmann Toys: The History of E P Lehmann 1881–1981* (New Cavendish Books, undated; ISBN 0 904568 40 7)

Fowler and Horsley, *Collins CDT (Technology)* (Collins Educational, 1988; ISBN 0 00327 434 9)

Hillier, M., *Automata and Mechanical Toys* (Jupiter Books, 1976; ISBN 904041 328; Bloomsbury Books, 1998; ISBN 1 87063 0270)

Hulten, P. and Tinguely, J., *A Magic Stronger Than Death* (Thames and Hudson, 1987; ISBN 0 50027 489 4)

Ives, Rob, *Cardboard Engineering Source Book* (Flying Pig, 2002; ISBN 0 95428 510 7)

Levy, A. (ed.), *The Great Toys of Georges Carette* (New Cavendish Books, 1975; ISBN 0 904568 02 4)

Lipman, J., *Calder's Universe* (Viking, New York, in co-operation with the Whitney Museum of American Art, 1976; ISBN 0670 19966 4)
   Showing Calder's 'Circus' in detail.

Marchand, F., *The History of Martin Mechanical Toys* (English edition) (Editions L'Automobiliste 1987; ISBN 2 86941 040 9)

Onn, A.L. and Alexander, G., *Cabaret Mechanical Movement* (Cabaret Mechanical Theatre, 1998; ISBN 0 9528729 0 0)
   See also Cabaret's website at www.cabaret.co.uk

Peppé, R., *Rodney Peppé's Moving Toys: With Complete Plans for Every Toy* (Evans Brothers Ltd, 1980; ISBN 0 237 449668)

Peppé, R., *Automata and Mechanical Toys* (The Crowood Press, 2002; ISBN 1 86126 510 7)

Peppé, R., *Toys and Models* (Antique Collectors Club, 2003; ISBN 1 85149 435 9)

Spilhaus, A. and K., *Mechanical Toys: How Old Toys Work* (Robert Hale, 1998; ISBN 0 7090 3857 7)

Spooner, P., *Spooner's Moving Animals* (Virgin, 1986; ISBN 0 86369 175 7) (published by Abrams in USA)

Tate Gallery Exhibition Catalogue, *Tinguely* (Tate Gallery Publications Department, 1982; ISBN 0 905005 78 3)

Basic Machines and How They Work (Dover Publications, 1971; ISBN 0 48621 709 4)

Conversion Table

Imperial and metric conversion table. Comparative dimensions: English–American (Imperial) and metric

Inches into millimetres

1/16in	=	1.6mm
1/8in	=	3.2mm
3/16in	=	4.7mm
1/4in	=	6.4mm
5/16in	=	7.9mm
3/8in	=	9.5mm
7/16in	=	11.1mm
1/2in	=	12.7mm
9/16in	=	14.3mm
5/8in	=	15.9mm
11/16in	=	17.5mm
3/4in	=	19.1mm
13/16in	=	20.6mm
7/8in	=	22.2mm
15/16in	=	23.8mm
1in	=	25mm
1 1/4in	=	32mm
1 1/2in	=	38mm
1 3/4in	=	44mm
2in	=	51mm
2 1/4in	=	57mm
2 1/2in	=	64mm
2 3/4in	=	70mm
3in	=	76mm
3 1/4in	=	82mm
3 1/2in	=	89mm
3 3/4in	=	95mm
4in	=	102mm
4 1/4in	=	108mm
4 1/2in	=	115mm
4 3/4in	=	121mm
5in	=	127mm
5 1/4in	=	133mm
5 1/2in	=	140mm
5 3/4in	=	146mm
6in	=	152mm
6 1/4in	=	158mm
6 1/2in	=	165mm
6 3/4in	=	171mm
7in	=	178mm
7 1/4in	=	184mm
7 1/2in	=	191mm
7 3/4in	=	197mm
8in	=	203mm
8 1/4in	=	209mm
8 1/2in	=	216mm
8 3/4in	=	222mm
9in	=	229mm
9 1/4in	=	235mm
9 1/2in	=	242mm
9 3/4in	=	248mm
10in	=	254mm
10 1/4in	=	260mm
10 1/2in	=	267mm
10 3/4in	=	273mm
11in	=	280mm
11 1/4in	=	285mm
11 1/2in	=	292mm
11 3/4in	=	298mm
12in	=	305mm
13in	=	330mm
14in	=	356mm
15in	=	381mm
16in	=	407mm
17in	=	432mm
18in	=	457mm
19in	=	483mm
20in	=	508mm
21in	=	534mm
22in	=	559mm
23in	=	584mm
24in	=	610mm
25in	=	635mm
26in	=	661mm
27in	=	686mm
28in	=	711mm
29in	=	737mm
30in	=	762mm
40in	=	1,016mm
50in	=	1,270mm
60in	=	1,525mm
70in	=	1,779mm
80in	=	2,033mm
90in	=	2,287mm
100in	=	2,540mm

Feet into metres

1ft	=	0.3m
2ft	=	0.6m
3ft	=	0.9m
4ft	=	1.2m
5ft	=	1.5m
6ft	=	1.8m
7ft	=	2.1m
8ft	=	2.4m
9ft	=	2.7m
10ft	=	3.05m
20ft	=	6.1m
30ft	=	9.1m
40ft	=	12.2m
50ft	=	15.2m
60ft	=	18.1m
70ft	=	21.3m
80ft	=	24.4m
90ft	=	27.4m
100ft	=	30.5m
200ft	=	61m
300ft	=	91m
400ft	=	122m
500ft	=	152m
600ft	=	183m
700ft	=	213m
800ft	=	244m
900ft	=	274m
1,000ft	=	304.8m

Millimetres into Inches

1mm	=	0.04in
2mm	=	0.08in
3mm	=	0.12in
4mm	=	0.16
5mm	=	0.20in
6mm	=	0.24in
7mm	=	0.28in
8mm	=	0.32in
9mm	=	0.36in
10mm	=	0.4in
11mm	=	0.43in
12mm	=	0.47in
13mm	=	0.51in
14mm	=	0.55in
15mm	=	0.59in
16mm	=	0.63in
17mm	=	0.67in
18mm	=	0.71in
19mm	=	0.75in
20mm	=	0.79in
21mm	=	0.83in
22mm	=	0.87in
23mm	=	0.91in
24mm	=	0.95in
25mm	=	0.98in
26mm	=	1.02in
27mm	=	1.06in
28mm	=	1.10in
29mm	=	1.14in
30mm	=	1.18in
31mm	=	1.22in
32mm	=	1.26in
33mm	=	1.3in
34mm	=	1.34in
35mm	=	1.38in
36mm	=	1.42in
37mm	=	1.46in
38mm	=	1.5in
39mm	=	1.54in
40mm	=	1.58in
45mm	=	1.77in
50mm	=	1.97in
55mm	=	2.17in
60mm	=	2.36in
65mm	=	2.56in
70mm	=	2.76in
75mm	=	2.95in
80mm	=	3.15in
85mm	=	3.35in
90mm	=	3.54in
95mm	=	3.75in
100mm	=	3.75in
125mm	=	4.92in
150mm	=	5.9in
175mm	=	6.89in
200mm	=	7.87in
225mm	=	8.86in
250mm	=	9.84in
275mm	=	10.83in
300mm	=	11.81in
325mm	=	12.8in
350mm	=	13.78in
375mm	=	14.77in
400mm	=	15.75in
425mm	=	16.74in
450mm	=	17.72in
475mm	=	18.71in
500mm	=	19.69in
525mm	=	20.67in
550mm	=	21.65in
575mm	=	22.64in
600mm	=	23.62in
625mm	=	24.61in
650mm	=	25.59in
675mm	=	26.57in
700mm	=	27.56in
750mm	=	29.53in
800mm	=	31.5in
850mm	=	33.46in
900mm	=	35.43in
950mm	=	37.4in
1,000mm	=	39.4in

Metres into feet and inches

1m	=	3ft 3 3/8in
2m	=	6ft 6 3/4in
3m	=	9ft 10in
4m	=	13ft 1 1/2in
5m	=	16ft 5in
6m	=	19ft 8in
7m	=	22ft 11 1/2in
8m	=	26ft 3in
9m	=	29ft 6 1/2in
10m	=	32ft 10in
20m	=	65ft 7in
30m	=	98ft 5in
40m	=	131ft 3in
50m	=	164ft
60m	=	197ft
70m	-	230ft
80m	=	262ft
90m	=	295ft
100m	=	328ft
200m	=	656ft
300m	=	984ft
400m	=	1312ft
500m	=	1640ft
600m	=	1968ft
700m	=	2297ft
800m	=	2615ft
900m	=	2953ft
1,000m	=	3281ft

INDEX